Blair's Britain

By the same author:

Spectators on the Shore
In Breaking Waves
Outer Charting
The Earthquake lands
The Stonehenge Syndrome

Souvenir

Admiral Harvey
Lord of the Californian

The Colonel's Tiger
Telepath's Dance

Who pays for protection (with Tracey Horton)
Return of the Heroes

Claude de Bernales: The Magnificent Miner
Richter's Laws

Blair's Britain

British Culture Wars and New Labour

by

Hal GP Colebatch

The Claridge Press

First published in Great Britain in 1999

by The Claridge Press
33 Canonbury Park South
London
N1 2 JW

Copyright © Hal G P Colebatch

Printed by
Antony Rowe Ltd
Chippenham

CIP data for this title is available from the British Library

ISBN No: 1-870626-27-3

Politics

Contents

Note

It may be noted that "conservative" here refers to a set of attitudes and values and "Conservative" refers to the Conservative Party.

Acknowledgements and Thanks

Some of this material has previously been published in *The Salisbury Review* (London) and *The Adelaide Review* (Adelaide, South Australia). While the opinions expressed remain my own, I am also indebted to those who contributed to discussions of parts of earlier drafts at functions organised by Merrie Cave and Donald Moore. My thanks are due as always to my beloved wife Alexandra for her unfailing help and support.

Chapter 1 Cultural Combatants

Conservative thought tends to see nations and societies as organic bodies of shared traditions and values.

Edmund Burke wrote in *Letters on a Regicide Peace*: "A Nation is a moral essence, not a geographical arrangement."

This is one definition of "culture." Another, by Left cultural historian Raymond Williams in *The Long Revolution*, is: "a particular way of life, which expresses certain meanings and values not only in art and learning but also in institutions and ordinary behaviour." This has been paraphrased as a "structure of feeling". G K Chesterton in *The Thing* called it with characteristically original insight, "The mental thrift of our fathers."

Tony Blair is not the first British Prime Minister to endorse these observations. He is, however, the first to see that moral essence or structure of feeling, that inheritance, as something to be changed by deliberate strategic action. He leads the first major post-Cold War government and the first government of any major Anglomorph country to launch a *specifically* cultural war, though others have done so incidentally. Its objectives go far beyond entrenching New Labour in power.

They encompass changing the identity of the country and the mental landscape and values of those who inhabit it. The destruction of Britain's links with its past and with its traditional culture seem under New Labour and the present cultural hegemony both a political strategy and an obsession. It is, however, important to bear in mind that the government is responding to certain social and cultural conditions as well as creating or trying to create them.

The relations between government, economic power and culture are complex: New Labour inherited and benefited from a certain cultural as well as economic climate. Now, to an unprecedented degree, it seeks to entrench a certain élite or Nomenklatura on the commanding heights of cultural power and exclude and silence that part of British culture seen as politically hostile. This is to be done by a wide alliance of political, media, artistic, financial and other interests.

Thus the fundamental issues in British politics today do not look like those of the past and often do not look political at all. The Italian Marxist Antonio Gramsci said that:

> Any revolutionary class, in addition to seizing political power, must secure *cultural* hegemony ... To seal its victory, such a class ... must challenge and oust [its enemies] in the realms of religion, philosophy, art, morality, language and manners.[1]

It would be hard to encapsulate more neatly New Labour's agendas, objectives and strategy. New Labour and the Nomenklatura are not monoliths, but they are given structure and coherence by a specific *Weltenschauung* which amounts to a virtual ideology.

A trade-off between the managerialist part of New Labour and the Left, with the Left being given cultural hegemony in exchange for its removal from economic levers, has been suggested. This says the same thing: to give the Left power in culture is to acquiesce and agree with such power. In any event cultural and economic power cannot be entirely separated. Chesterton in *The Flying Inn* and John Buchan in *The Three Hostages* were two among many who wrote that British traditional polity could not defend itself against the English leader with an UnEnglish mind.

New Labour is uniquely positioned for cultural revolution. It came to power free not only from the social disciplines and, to an extent, the military alliances of the Cold War, but also from much of the traditional power of the big unions and the ideological baggage of socialism, and with a majority large enough to make questions of "mandate" irrelevant.

Old Labour in a hundred years of traditional politics had made only limited political gains and its periods of government had been short and not particularly successful. In the 1980s it seemed the Party of outdated, doomed reactionism.

However, the end of the Cold War, the discrediting of socialism, the apparent loss of nerve by, and faith in, all manner of conservative institutions, and by no means least the gift of a booming economy, had cleared the way for a new kind of political conflict.

Between 1992 and 1997 the Conservatives managed the economy well and left it stronger than at any time since modern economic patterns emerged, and the British standard of living at its highest ever. Their reward was to lose four and a half million votes from what had seemed, for the four previous elections, a fairly steady electoral base of between 13 and 14 million.[2] The succession of relatively minor scandals involving Conservative MPs could not alone account for this, particularly in an age which prided itself on its permissiveness. There were deeper cultural factors at work.

Further, with 43% of the vote converted into 63% of the Seats in Parliament (although with the lowest voter turnout since 1935 — fewer than one eligible citizen in three voted Labour), Britain was at least temporarily a One-Party State. It appears this result was achieved partly through tactical voting and the Referendum Party splitting the anti-Labour vote, but, fundamentally, not through a great increase in Labour support as much as through a huge failure among traditional conservative voters to support Conservative Party candidates. New Labour looked both safe and an idea whose time had come.

It has been said Labour won when, and because, it seemed there was no chance it would do anything radical. In 1992 the tired and divided Conservatives had retained office against a

Labour Party which still had some socialist vocabulary (the Conservatives then received a larger number of votes than did Labour in 1997). Tony Blair, on the other hand, did not even pretend to be a socialist or of the Left. Other threatening aspects of Leftism were also gone. The State was seen as in retreat with widespread privatisation, Union power was greatly weakened, Communist or pro-Soviet infiltration of the Labour Party was no longer an issue, and what had once been the Red Army scavenged for food on Russian rubbish-tips.

Post-Cold War current affairs in the old sense of international relations seemed to arouse mainly boredom, be they television images of NATO jets in the Balkans or starving babies in Africa. Newspapers across the spectrum had never been more relentlessly banal: it seemed as if even in the middle-market papers an article on nuclear proliferation in the Indian subcontinent might appear only when the absence of one of the innumerable gossip-writers had left a hole.

Blair has commonly been depicted as a centrist — almost non-political — politician, certainly the least radical of politicians, a "chipper apolitical imp"[3], in one paper, "startlingly unradical" according to political writer Edward Pearce[4], or as the *Economist* put it, "The Strangest Tory Ever Sold", a managerialist leading a meritocratic government which had discarded virtually all the shibboleths of socialism. Labour MP Bob Marshall-Andrews has been quoted as saying:

> New Labour has no time for political philosophy. In our modern, pluralist, classless, Ford-Galaxy-driving society, such things are old Hattersley.[5]

Paul Johnson claimed that:

> In essentials, Blair's Government is a continuation of Margaret Thatcher's after the hiatus of the John Major interregnum.[6]

I have heard similar views expressed repeatedly in Britain, not least in Conservative Clubs. An important part of the style of Blairism is inclusiveness, with Liberal Democrat leader Paddy Ashdown and former Tory leader John Major brought very publicly into the fold for various purposes. Although New Labour was elected by a minority of the vote and an even smaller minority of the voting population, Blair suggests it embodies a national consensus of proper-thinking people. David Marquand has written:

> In place of the Thatcherite cold shower, it offers a warm bath, administered by a hegemonic people's party appealing equally to every part of the nation.[7]

Stewart Steven claimed:

> [Blair] thinks the ideological approach to politics was almost a perversion of the 20th Century.[8]

There is also an official version. The British High Commissioner to Australia, Alex Allen, told an Australian audience:

> Britain is a buzzing, exciting place spreading out in many areas of manufacturing and industry, in creative design and cutting-edge technology ... Blair is leading a third wave, between free markets and the traditional socialist approach... He did not say what the Tories had done was bad, he agreed to build on them. New Labour is very different from traditional labour ...[9]

In 1997 both the old Right and the old Left had lost what defined and gave legitimacy to their values. The old Right has seen the apparent great weakening of such social and moral certainties as monarchism, patriotism, and military and civil values like honour, pride, dignity and tradition; the old Left has lost Communism, the Soviet Union, the KGB and its fronts such as the "peace" movements, the Gulag as an eventual destination for opponents, and hope of political power through revolution. The socialists have lost socialism and the labour market has been radically transformed. Although neo-Nazis were visible in Europe, neo-Nazis in Britain either disappeared, or — which came to the same thing — were the subject of a media blackout (rock-music and the soccer hooligan culture were perhaps a kind of equivalent or substitute). Groups like the Workers' Revolutionary Party had disappeared apart from a few forlorn and smudgy newsletters. Across the traditional political spectrum there seemed to be a great quiet. Neither Right or Left would abandon the pursuit of power, but the vocabulary and cosmetics associated with the exercise — and therefore in fact the whole of the culture — would be different in future.

Even on University campuses, Marxism and socialism were old hat. As one academic friend put it, with a memorably mixed metaphor, "The wave of the 60's has burnt itself out." University Leftist manifestos seemed to have dwindled to demands for free courses. Economic debate had hardly ever been more muted. By discarding Leftism in this climate, according to conventional wisdom, Blair captured not only something called the middle ground of politics, but also the conservative ground.

These things are all in a sense true. They also disguise deeper and opposite truths. New Labour came to power at a time when social and cultural conditions were in a state of extraordinary liquidity. The Conservative Major Government had done little or nothing to foster conservatism in a social or cultural sense, and the Thatcher Government was perceived (perhaps incorrectly in the case of Margaret Thatcher herself) as being preoccupied with a free-market ideology which was narrowly focussed on economics and at odds with many aspects of traditional conservative culture, traditions and values. Indeed it is hard to think of any recent Conservative administrations notable for concern for the preservation of conservative culture. International mass culture was largely the product of certain aspects of American culture.

One result of this was that New Labour came to power at a time when Britain was suffering from a widespread loss of historical memory, and spokesmen for traditional culture in all its aspects were isolated and discounted. New culture and new governmant came together.

One of the most perceptive descriptions of Blair's and New Labour's real ideology has been "radical centrist". Blair is, in fact, not the least but the most radical British Prime Minister since the office emerged in its modern form. Previous Prime Ministers wished to keep power as long as possible but by-and-large accepted that there would always be an Opposition and it would win government from time to time. In their more objective or philosophical moments they might have reflected that this was healthy. New Labour has nothing to do with such notions. Blair told the 1997 Labour Party Conference that: "I want the 21st century to be the century of radicals."[10]

This can, first, be seen in the political and constitutional sphere. In New Labour's first year evidence accumulated that the Executive despised Parliament and sought to degrade it. The Scottish and Welsh Devolution referenda were plebiscites in advance of Parliamentary debate: Parliament would have to debate legislation with the knowledge that Devolution was a *fait accompli*, and the Executive could use the huge Labour majority to rubber-stamp any arrangement. By the end of New Labour's first year in office Parliament seemed a shade and government was by Executive statement. There had not even been a debate over so important a question as the expansion of NATO. In June, 1998, it appeared British armed forces might be committed against Serbia over Kosovo without debate. Prime Minister's Question Time was reduced and the whole institution of Parliamentary Questions down-graded. By July, 1998, the Prime Minister had voted 14 times in 325 divisions.[11] Government policy announcements came increasingly to be through press-statements and leaks to favoured journalists (There were reports of more independent-minded journalists being subjected not only to discrimination but to intimidation).

The unwritten nature of the Constitution has been seen as a guarantee of Parliamentary soverignty (one remembers the truism of first-year political science courses: "The British Parliament *could* pass laws that condemn every red-haired man in the country to death — but of course it *wouldn't*"), but in the absence of more defined checks and balances the product of a degraded and impotent Parliament could be expanded or even unlimited Executive power.

Blair and New Labour appeared to favour an Executive-*appointed* Upper House. While it is a complex question, the peculiarities of the unwritten British Constitution with its heavy reliance on convention and "structure of feeling" seem at least at first sight to make this feasible. Nowhere else in the major Anglomorph countries in modern times has there been a proposed expansion of Executive power on such a scale. While like all analogies this is inexact, it is possible to imagine the political earthquake if a US President sought to amend the US Constitution to give himself power to appoint the Senate. Impeachment would be the least of it.

In Australia also, there have been checks and balances on Executive power which do not appear to exist in Britain. In 1975 the Whitlam Government, which had some ideological similarities to Blairism, and which had set out to test the Constitution to its limits by the expansion of Executive powers including the notorious "21 Bills," was dismissed by the Governor-General following a series of crises, and an election was called. However, the written Australian Constitution provided for this, and the Governor-General's action though politically controversial was plainly legal. A British Prime Minister being dismissed and an election called by the Monarch is practically unthinkable (Further, Australia has an upper house, the Senate, which is elected on a different basis to the lower house, not appointed by the Executive, and which can have considerable real independence). Nor, despite certain other vexed problems, could there have been remotely equivalent attempts to expand Executive power in Canada or New Zealand without major crises and destabilisation.

One can, in fact, see, in aspects of New Labour's intimate relationship with major money and "cultural" interests as well as unions, aspects of the Corporate State associated with Mussolinin's imperfectly realised theories of Fascism. This is combined with obvious and undisguised disdain for the traditional institutions of Parliament.[12]

However, the political and Constitutional questions are only the beginning of the matter. New Labour has a complex relationship with, on one hand a pervading "high" culture with a strong element of Nihilism — a media-arts-entertainment-fashion complex apparently emphasising ugliness, moral baseness, and death as entertainment, and on the other a proletarianised culture revolving around rock-music, spectator sport, sentimentality and bodily functions. These two cultures meet at an increasing number of points, crushing traditional culture in a pincer-movement. This is certainly not to say the cultural Nomenklatura cannot criticise New Labour — it can and does — but that New Labour's behaviour suggests it thinks the transformation of public culture a prime weapon in the destruction of Old Britain and its associated conservative traditions and values. Stephen Glover has remarked:

> Marx thought that the proletariat would replace the bourgeoisie just as the bourgeoisie had replaced the aristocracy. In an economic sense this hasn't happened ... and yet our shared culture is increasingly proletarian ... So I suppose it is true to say that in one sense Marx was right. Proletarian values rule, OK.[13]

This was also a time when conventional and traditional moral codes, values, beliefs and ways of behaving had been under unprecedented attack — or rather, when attacks on them had

become unprecedentedly pervasive throughout the entire culture. The political and cultural aspects of New Labour and New
Britannia might, in contemplating one another, join in quota-
tion of Rupert Brooke:

> Now God be thanked Who has matched us with His hour,
> And caught our youth, and wakened us from sleeping ...

While the cultural style of the government itself has been been
fairly consistent within its own terms, its policies have been full
of ambiguities and contradictions. While Blair himself and some
of those close to him projected a pragmatic, almost apolitical
image, throughout the government, public sector, armed forces,
media, churches and academe, the culture of political correctness was probably more powerful than ever (It was not an apolitical act for a public authority to distribute contraceptives to
13-year-olds). Not only were the beliefs, value-systems and
agenda of New Labour hard to pin down, but it was an open
question how far its people were consciously aware of what they
were doing. There were, however, vague and ambiguous refer-
ences to something called "The Project" which at least suggest
the existence of an inner circle (not, it appears coinciding with
the Parliamentary Party) that does have a clear strategic agenda
and knows what it is doing.

Throughout New Labour one sees a strange blend of old
and new ideologies and notions. Blair himself remains curiously
nebulous, his most politically useful characteristic being a considerable ability to project reassurance, and to use language in
which the same words convey different messages to different
audiences and with which it is difficult to disagree.

He claims to oppose abortion but has consistently voted for
it; he has claimed to support traditional institutions of marriage,
but the budget of March, 1998, contained incentives to substitute work for welfare and reduced the Marriage Allowance.
The combined effects of these measures, but particularly the

latter, would be to increase the number of illegitimate births and force mothers further out of the role of home-makers, the obvious results being more parentless children; he has spoken in favour of conventional family life but he and New Labour overwhelmingly supported a Bill to lower the age for legal homosexual relations to 16 — a move opposed even by the Anglican church and described in the *Catholic Herald* as marking "a new low in this country's slide into moral degeneracy;"[14] he has been a CND supporter but committed Britain, almost alone, to military action with the United States against Iraq. It is far easier to say what, politically, Blair is not than what he is: he is not socialist, conservative, or liberal.

Christianity is an ambiguous and problematical feature of New Labour. Blair, a nominal Anglican, has raised speculation that he is attracted to Catholicism by going to Mass in Westminster Cathedral, but has said nothing publicly about it, despite the fact his religion is of more public and political importance for several reasons than would be the case with a private citizen. He has reasserted effective Prime Ministerial control of Anglican Episcopal appointments. Blair and four other senior Ministers — Chancellor Gordon Brown, Home Secretary Jack Straw, Culture Minister Chris Smith and public service Minister David Clark — are members of the Christian Socialist Movement, a group which marked its opposition to traditional values by appointing a lesbian as chief executive.[15] His own family life seems almost anachronistically conventional and bourgeois.

Labour in Opposition pushed amendments to the Conservative Government's Family Law Act to fund "marriage support" agencies but in government removed funding for half of these.[16] The same day one newspaper reported that the government wanted Britain's doctors to warn children of the dangers of sexual promiscuity[17], another reported that the Blairs had been the guests at a "discreet dinner party" of that less than spotless exemplar of clean living, Mr Mick Jagger[18].

Blairism shows an affinity with the rock-music culture celebrating drug-taking, law-breaking and physical violence and aggression, as well as occasional suggestions of a kind of commercial Satanism. Blair himself appears indifferent to the classical musical and other Western cultural traditions. As music-writer Norman Lebrecht put it, New Labour by embracing rock-music, associated itself with behaviour that scorned law, public safety and generally accepted standards of common decency. He continued:

> By attaching "serious value" to popular music, New Labour does not only mean financial worth. It sees pop as a model for New Britain and some camp followers — including, it seems, HM Chief Inspector of Schools — would like Britpop to be taught in schools. But what educational worth is there in an activity that thrives on abusing core values?...[19]

While Blair exudes a certain sense of considering himself of the Elect, he betrays little real interest in anything beyond politics except rock-music, modernism, and the penumbra of 1960s cultural values that make up the official creed of New Britain. In the Labour Government's agenda details, even of matters such as European integration and the future of the United Kingdom, somehow disappear on close inspection. Education policies do not seem to reveal any overall thrust, being full of contradictions between meritocracy and old socialism.

Plans have been announced for two new and larger aircraft-carriers but these will not, apparently, be ready for 14 years, and with even their commencement years away it is hard to know how serious the announcement is. Such plans have been announced before and fallen victim to defence "reviews". Will future governments really consider such enormous expenditure really justified to enable Britain to tag along behind America in intervening in remote possible-stops in which, apart from the Middle East and the Falklands, vital British interests are unlikely to be affected? In any case, when such large ships spend a lot of time undergoing maintenance and refits, one wonders how viable a two-carrier navy is for a major power.

The slashing of the Territorial Army from 58,000 to 40,000 announced in 1998 seemed to herald the loss of a very cost-effective way of integrating the Army into society and providing very socially useful training and discipline, and which also provided a variety of technical training and gave paid part-time work which also mitigated the effects of unemployment for many people. The Army's generally culturally conservative traditions and values presumably have a good deal to do with this particular cut. The Navy and Air Force reserves also virtually disappeared.

On the home front there seemed to be a strain of uncaring inhumanity, or at least a feeling that many social problems were out of control or could not or did not need to be tackled. Horrific prison conditions have been documented in detail but there seems to be little if any interest in prison reform or efficient policing (I have visited a number of minimum, medium and maximum-security prisons frequently in Australia and while they are certainly not garden areas, inmates' lives are seldom in danger). The utterly failed experiment of turning mentally-ill people, some highly dangerous to themselves and others, into the streets, has been carried on and only in July 1998 was a vague campaign to eventually have some of the homeless placed in hostel care announced. Ragged and stinking women with infant children could be seen begging in London tube stations, apparently without government intervention on their or the children's behalf. Certainly some of these conditions had been inherited from the previous government but this was no real reason for continuing inaction.

Bruce Anderson has written:

> But this government is not about policy details or about strategy;

its social programme is a magpie's nest of improvisation and
theft. For the Blair government, the medium is the message,
and the message is Mr Blair himself. Mr Blair not only
dominates his government to an extent greater than any
previous PM did, including Mrs Thatcher; he is its *raison d'être*;
his personality is its philosophy.[20]

Anderson pointed to the change in Blair's attitude to fox-hunting when it was shown to be supported by a large and well-
organised lobby: before the election, one or two would-be Tory
defectors lobbied him, offering their support if he would spare
their sport. The offer was contemptuously dismissed, for there
would be no place for hunting in New Britain. After the countryside march in March, 1998, showed the strength of support
for fox-hunting, the anti-hunting Bill was allowed to die in Parliament. Blair, as usual, failed to attend to support the vote, and
anti-hunting protesters were ejected from the public gallery amid
plaintive cries that "Blair promised!" (He was reported to have
promised to vote for the Bill in an interview published in the
RSPCA magazine *Animal Action* the previous September, before
opposition to the Bill became organised.)

Blair defended his campaign to "rebrand" Britain with the
claim that:

> We are forging a new patriotism based on the potential we can
> fulfil in the future. There is an energy about Britain at the
> moment...[21]

Taxed by some unkind commentators with the fact that this
statement was meaningless, Blair went further in the *Daily Mail*
of 3 April, 1998, with two columns under the heading "Why
our image DOES matter." He claimed in this that he wanted
Britain to be seen as a "vibrant, modern place" because "countries wrapped in nostalgia cannot build a strong future. You
cannot be backward in coming forward in today's global mar-

ket place." This claimed:

> Our history, our sense of occasion, pride in pageantry — these
> are vital parts of what we stand for, but we cannot be defined
> by our past alone ... We have a dynamic future as well as a
> proud past ... I'm not talking about the whims of fashion but
> the long-term confidence and prosperity of a nation that has a
> great history to celebrate and a great future to build.

Where had one heard stuff like this before? About 30 years ago
Peter Sellers put out a record lampooning a political speech of
clichés such as:

> We must build, but we must build *surely*.

The axiom is attributed to Sun Tzu that the most difficult enemy to attack is the one who, like water, presents no shape. Blair
has confounded critics by presenting himself in no form that fits
the terms of the old political vocabulary.

Nebulousness has also been a feature of foreign policy. This
coincides with the fact that, for the first time since its emergence
as a modern nation, Britain seems to have no serious foreign
role. With the prospect of integration into a Franco-German
dominated Europe, and the simultaneous and related apparent
break-up of the Union, Britain appears to be sleepwalking away
from National sovereignty. Here too a lack of fundamental seriousness is reflected both in government policies and in a general, pervasive cultural climate. Minor and symbolic foreign
policy matters seem to command far more government/media
attention than such matters as the fate of democracy in Russia.
Britain's victory in the World Cup over a small third-world country, Tunisia, and its defeat by Columbia and Argentina, commanded intense official as well as media attention (it is only a
fairly recent development that football should be considered a
Prime Minister's business at all).

Blair claimed that, as a result of Britain's leading role at the 1997 Commonwealth Heads of Government Meeting, "tough" sanctions would be imposed on the dictatorship in Nigeria. He did not say exactly *when* this would happen. Sanctions had been decided on two years previously and nothing had been done. The problem of seeking to lead the Commonwealth while simultaneously abandoning it for Europe was ignored. A "special relationship" with Russia was briefly touted but proved instantly illusionary.

With the Government obsessed with the significance of style, symbols and attitudes, it was also notable that in January, 1998, Foreign Secretary Robin Cook refused to meet China's leading human rights campaigner, Wei Jingshen, shortly before he himself was due to visit China. The indifference to human rights this behaviour indicated was compounded by the excuse offered: that there was "no time" for a meeting which need have taken only a few minutes.[22] In February, 1998, the European Union, of which Britain held the presidency, decided not to table or co-sponsor a draft resolution condemning civil rights violations in China. Britain ceased the practice of the preceding nine years — dating from the Tienanman Square massacre — of supporting a resolution on human rights in China at the UN Human Rights Commission. Blair told Parliament, without other explanation, that: "We did not feel that this UN resolution was the right way to proceed."[23] Cook had previously emphasised to an unprecedented degree the need for an ethical foreign policy. When the question was raised of Rupert Murdoch having allegedly interfered to prevent the publication of Chris Patten's book, which apparently criticised China, a matter the subject of Page-One furore in the broadsheet press and enormous television coverage, Blair contemptuously told Parliament that he "was not aware of the incident to which you refer".[24] However, in April, 1998, Blair himself, echoed by William Hague, publicly intervened with a statement on behalf of a woman imprisoned as a result of trusting a confidence trickster, and whose manifestly unjust sentence had convulsed the nation. The woman concerned was a fictitious character in a television soap-opera.

In science, environmentalism and "green" issues this nebulousness could also be seen. Rhetoric was vaguely green but the Housing Minister set out to reverse the protection which Green Belt legislation gave the rural environment, demanding initially that 4,400,000 new houses be built, largely in what remained of the countryside. Broadcaster Jonathan Dimbleby, president of the Soil Association, said this would make the countryside "a futuristic nightmare of suburbia unbounded" with the cities abandoned to "a vicious underclass which inhabits an urban wasteland that the wealthy have left behind." New Labour also promised to "buy more coal" at inflated prices to keep uneconomic coal mines open and a number of power-stations spewing coal-smoke.

To identify all this with an ideology seems strange. Nonetheless, a thing called Blairism can be recognised. It is not only the first truly post-Cold War but also perhaps post-Twentieth Century government in Britain.

Paddy Ashdown, speaking on the BBC on 30 May, 1998, hailed: "A new style of politics for a new Century". This may link with the Government's strange obsession with the Millennium Dome and the "Millennium Experience" in general. The Government may use this occasion, apart from bread-and-circuses and vote-buying with grants to strategically-placed interest-groups, to reinforce notions of the Twenty-First Century as a *tabula rasa* on which to write the new terms of politics and culture.

In 1982, Magnus Clarke, a lecturer in Social Sciences at Australia's Deakin University, suggested:

> A Society can be said to have survived if it is still recognisable, and collapse is used as a term to denote definite ending in the long *or* short term *when cultural identity is lost*.[25] [emphasis in original]

Shortly before his death in 1997 Isaiah Berlin observed that for the first time since 1789 the Left has no project in Europe. But, as Geoffrey Wheatcroft pointed out in his brilliant *Prospect* article[26], this should have been qualified as no large *political* project. *Kulturkampf* is another matter.

Stewart Steven has quoted Blair as having "hated it" when he went abroad as a young man and Americans would talk of Britain's glorious past "all those beefeaters and things". To attempt a psychological analysis on such a basis would be rash — and what one "hates" as a young person is frequently what is deep-down loved — but still this may be significant. The driving obsessions of radical political leaders in general seem closely linked to youthful experiences and emotions, associated with a gnawing sense of inferiority, which have settled deep in the psyche. If Blair is driven by obsessive hatred of Britain's past and compensatory desire to "modernise" beyond ordinary pragmatic changes, then this is a matter of profound importance. The shadowy concept of "The Project" certainly suggests a definite if secretive strategy with some kind of clear end and objective. Steven may have written more truly that he knew when he concluded with the observation that, after one year in Government, "The Blair revolution has barely begun."[27]

Footnotes

1 Gramsci, quoted by P Bassett, *Salisbury Review*, Spring 1998, p49.
2 Margaret Thatcher secured votes of 13.7 million, 13 million and 13.8 million. In the 1992 election when Thatcherism was still plainly an important factor, John Major secured 14.1 million.
3 *Mail on Sunday*, 1 March 1998.
4 *History Today*, June 1998, p 9.
5 *Mail on Sunday*, 1 February 1998.

6 *Daily Mail*, 27 March 1998.
7 The Blair Paradox, *Prospect*, May 1998, p 19.
8 *Daily Mail*, 26 April 1998.
9 *The West Australian*, 11 April 1998.
10 *Daily Telegraph*, 19 June 1998.
11 *Daily Telegraph*, 8 July 1998.
12 In this New Labour is to some extent recapitulating the experience of certain Australian Labor governments. The Labor government of Western Australia in 1983 soon acquired the nick-name "WA Inc" in reference to its Corporatist-Statist attitudes to real and imagined money power and other so-called peak groups. It collapsed in a welter of scandals and criminal prosecutions. There were similar experiences in other States.
13 *Daily Telegraph*, 6 March 1998.
14 *Daily Telegraph*, 27 June 1998.
15 *Daily Mail*, 26 January 1998.
16 *Daily Mail*, 23 March 1998.
17 *Mail on Sunday*, 18 January 1998.
18 *Sunday Telegraph*, 18 January 1998.
19 *Daily Telegraph*, 1 April 1998.
20 *The Spectator*, 14 March 1998.
21 *The Sunday Times*, 29 March 1998.
22 *Daily Telegraph*, 9 January 1998.
23 *Daily Telegraph*, 12 March 1998.
24 *Daily Telegraph*, 12 March 1998.
25 Magnus Clarke, *The Nuclear Destruction of Britain*, 1982, p 25.
26 Geoffrey Wheatcroft, Annus memorabilis, *Prospect*, January, 1998, p 25.
27 *Daily Mail*, 26 April 1998.

Chapter 2 Foxes and Honours

In April, 1998, an independent think-tank, the Social Affairs Unit, published a collection of essays, *Faking It: The Sentimentalisation of Modern Society*, criticising the Emotional Correctness with which New Britain had identified himself. A theme of one essay, by Professor Anthony O'Hear, a distinguished philosopher, was that the nation was neglecting values such as duty, self-sacrifice and restraint, and that the Dianamania was *ersatz* and manipulated. The Prime Minister interrupted a middle-east peace-making mission (his role inspired, he claimed, by the film *Schindler's List*[28]) to attack this "unadulterated snobbery"[29] and to claim: "I honestly can't understand the reason for insulting people's feelings like that."[30] He continued: "Diana's power is [*sic*] born out of emotion and there's nothing wrong with that."[31] His spokesman, Alistair Campbell, claimed that Professor O'Hear was a "right-wing, old-fashioned snob."[32]

That a Prime Minister and his spokesman, a public employee, should do this showed both Blair's sensitivity to criticism of his own cultural iconography and an assumption that it was proper for him to use his position to intervene in private social and academic debate. This was a *diktat* for Emotional Correctness. It is hard to imagine any previous British Prime Minister doing such a thing. A favourable biography of Princess Diana by a well-known progressive female journalist published a few weeks later, which attacked the Royal Family in the most extreme and abusive terms, provoked no such rebuke.

The use by the Prime Minister of the present tense to describe the dead Princess's "power" was strange, suggesting that he saw it as an ongoing ally. And was there a certain echo in the Prime Ministerial use of those words: "power is born out of emotion"? What could it be? ... "The Triumph of the Will? ..."

About the same time the Prime Minister issued a statement as to how saddened he and his wife were by the death of "Linda", that is to say Lady Paul McCartney, who had allegedly "made a tremendous contribution across a whole range of public life". The Blairs had never actually met Lady McCartney, although Mrs Blair said that they had been planning to do so. He also told the Egyptians that sphinxes and pyramids, like British castles and pageantry, offered an "incomplete picture" of the country (many Egyptians are very proud of the pyramids). Less than a week later he intervened in the Mary Bell affair to dictate the emotionally correct line (which again coincided with that of the tabloid press). Keith Waterhouse wrote of this:

> He was expressing public opinion, or anyway public bar opinion, for which he has an unerring instinct. The line was not as inspired as his catch-in-the-throat soundbite about the People's Princess a few months ago, but once more he hit the nail on the head ... Where is our sense of proportion going?
>
> Tony Blair was the conduit for the near-hysteria attending the Princess Di tragedy. He is the conduit for the rage surrounding Mary Bell. "She must be found, named and shamed" said one of the victim's mothers in her understandable distress. But was that the time for Tony to stick his oar in or for his sidekick to say she had brought it on herself? Was it their function to fuel the fury? Is this their New Britain? ...[34]

On the death of Frank Sinatra, Blair claimed: "I have grown up with Frank Sinatra and he will be deeply missed." The *Sunday Telegraph* commented: "Frank's death, you see, was not just about Frank. It was about how Tony related to Frank."[35] Following press outrage at football hooliganism, the Prime Minister made a strange, illegal, suggestion, presumably again in line with public-bar opinion, that football hooligans be sacked from their jobs, although he was a lawyer and his wife was a highly-paid specialist in employment law.

International Development Minister Claire Short, a member of the Old Left, had claimed:

> The quality of discussion about public life has deteriorated to such an extent that the public is now utterly cynical. Politics becomes murky and disgusting. Something has gone horribly, horribly wrong ... It's not just dumbing down, it's a sort of crassness.[36]

Sir Terence Conran wrote in the *Times Magazine* encouraging the chef Marco Pierre White, to "Be a man of the people. Be a Blairite." The *Times* commented of this injunction:

> He was not discussing welfare reform, but *foie gras* in *pigeon de Bresse*. Sir Terence felt that, in reality, "what we are talking about is democracy", which is, Tom Paine and Martin Luther King might have been grateful to know, "offering good food in enjoyable surroundings to rich and poor". The huddled masses queuing at Quaglino's for a *plateau de fruits de mer* (at £27.50 per person) must be grateful that they are playing their part in the emancipation of mankind.[37]

Meanwhile, an 81-year-old crippled war veteran, refused a place in a care home by a local authority, committed suicide by throwing himself under a train. The coroner was told he had been taunted by youths for being an ex-soldier. On the day he died, he had visited the local British Legion Club and had asked friends for help. He had 63 pence in his bank book and could not pay his bus fare home.[38]

However, the time was happier for some: it was reported that the Foreign Office Minister, Derek Patchett, spent £2,500

of taxpayers' money taking his wife abroad on government business, which involved a 10-day-tour of Australia and the Pacific
islands. Lord Irvine, the Lord Chancellor, who will be mentioned again later, took his wife to Trinidad at tax-payer's ex-
pense, with a bill at the Hilton Hotel of £2,350. Foreign Secretary
Cook had rules on spousal travel reinterpreted so his mistress
rather than his wife could accompany him overseas on military
aircraft. The Minister for European Affairs also took his mistress. Ministers ran up foreign travel bills of about £1.4 million,
as well as about £8 million on entertaining and hospitality, in
the first five months of government. Each Cabinet Minister was
allowed two political advisors, at an annual cost to the taxpayer
of £2.6 million — nearly twice the amount on similar postings
in the last year of the Conservative government. The Prime Minister had 17 full-time advisors plus two aides for his wife (a bar-
rister in private practice reputed to earn more than £100,000
per year). This came to £849,000, double the amount spent by
John Major. Despite Mr and Mrs Blair each enjoying 6-figure
incomes, they also claimed more than £1,500 per year from the
tax-payer in child benefits.[39]

Fourteen Ministers were given the use of official houses. In
all, about £826,000 was spent on Ministerial grace-and-favour
homes. A London apartment was also given to the President of
the Board of Trade. Tennis Counts were upgraded at Cheq-
uers, the Prime Minister's country residence, and a designer
kitchen installed for him in London.[40] A Government spokesman said that it was "demeaning" for the Opposition to raise
these matters.

Another Old Labour figure, Baroness Castle, former Social
Security Minister, asked plaintively:

> What we want to know is: what kind of a society this Govern-
> ment is trying to create?[41]

The lesson of anthropology has been well learnt: like orangutans in a burning rain-forest, Conservatives and conservatives are to be destroyed not only by hunting but more importantly by the elimination of their eco-system. However this does not affect old Left and old Right equally: the old Left can be given their own reservations in the socio-political areas which matter to them, such as the Arts-Media-Entertainment-Academia complex, and possibly a geographical and political stronghold in Scotland, where, beyond a *cordon sanitaire*, their leaders can enjoy the fruits of office and the privileges of Statesmen. The cultural conservatives of the "Right" are slated for destruction.

In the first months of Blairism it became patent that the Executive was taking hold of levers of cultural power: when Blair revived the practice of personally approving the appointment of Church of England Bishops, Stuart Bell, Second Church Estates Commissioner and in effect the Government Minister for the Church of England, spelt out Labour's policy for the Church in an extraordinary speech to the General Synod in November, 1997. The Church, he directed, must "modernise and become closer to the people". The Church was to be turned into an instrument for refashioning consciousness. One Tory government after another had endured all manner of attacks from the Established Church and the virulently Leftist World Council of Churches and associated organisations, and would have been the subject of all manner of outcry if it had even appeared to intervene in Church affairs (The episode "Bishop's Gambit" in *Yes, Prime Minister*,though avoiding identifying the hapless fictional Prime Minister with any Party, brilliantly depicts the atmosphere of the old regime as the Prime Minister is presented with the choice of a Marxist or an atheist for bishop).

Lord Irvine demanded more "Labour" judicial appointments, and forecast "a very significant transfer of power to the judges" from Parliament. A Bill was introduced to incorporate the European Convention on Human Rights into British law, in effect forcing the courts into a political role. Details of government-

Nomenklatura interference in the media and the BBC (such as the Draper affair which broke in July, 1998), would occupy a book in themselves.

"Mo" Mowlam, the Northern Ireland Secretary, told *Hot Press*, the Dublin-based rock-music magazine, that the Royal Family should move out of Buckingham Palace. She followed this up by suggesting the Royal Family would have to conform to the culture of New Labour to survive:

> I said the Queen should move out [of Buckingham Palace] because I wanted [the Royal Family] to have a modern palace and make themselves representative of where we were at, rather than something that was representative of the past.

> That's what I still believe. And I hope that when one of the others takes over — ie Charles — that he does begin to adapt to what Blair represents as part of our culture. *If they can do that,* then they have a future.[42] [emphasis added]

This was headlined: "Mowlam tells Prince to follow Blair path or perish." It was an extraordinary statement from a Cabinet Minister. Certainly it showed the assumption of the possession of the *Zeitgeist*. The phrase "what Blair represents as part of our culture" was most significant and revealing. If, after that, conservatives did not realise the facts of the present *Kulturkampf*, they did not have much excuse.

The efforts to ban fox-hunting targeted cultural conservatism and values of traditional and historic patriotism. The widespread protests, culminating, with other rural grievances, in the countryside march on London in March, 1998, led the Government to let the Bill fail. However conflict over hunting gave another aspect of New Britain a chance to express itself. In December, 1997, a gang of more than 100 hunt saboteurs wearing terrorist-style black balaclavas and wielding iron bars, axe-handles and baseball bats, ambushed the Hursley Hambledon Hunt near Warnford in Hampshire. These were different to hunt saboteurs of yore: they were out to *really* get not only the riders but the spectators. One 25-year-old man, watching a hunt for the first time, was bludgeoned four times in the head. Scores of people were injured, including a woman and a baby in cars cut by broken glass when the saboteurs smashed the windows with baseball bats. Elderly men, women and children appeared to be special targets. A 62-year-old eye surgeon had bones in his face broken. One victim, a 49-year-old Naval Officer, who received three broken ribs when beaten with a pick-axe handle when trying to stop his wife's car being smashed up, said the attackers shouted: "The people have spoken!" A few weeks later men, women and children at the Puckeridge Hunt in Herefordshire were attacked and beaten up on three occasions by saboteurs who arrived in unmarked vans. One woman said: "They bounced my friend's car and tried to get it off the road. Then one man jumped into my car and grabbed my belongings. I was terrified." The man then ran off with the car-keys.[43] Following this there were a string of reports of isolated hunt followers, including uninvolved spectators, being set upon and beaten with metal bars and clubs.[44]

When I began sending press cuttings about the Britain of New Labour to a friend in Australia, he responded with the observation that it was a "new Puritanism". On reflection I saw that he was right. However it is a Puritanism of a strangely ambiguous kind. Michael Foster, who introduced the Bill to ban fox-hunting, is a competition angler, so his motive could hardly have been objection to animal suffering. That the opposition was not based on concern for foxes was made plain by leaders in the Labour-Leftish *Observer* and *Guardian*. The *Observer* of 1 March, 1998, said that:

> It is not so much the killing of foxes that concern those who want to see it banned. It is its ritualisation into an exclusive sport which commands a key role, albeit small, in our culture, that so many find offensive.

The *Guardian* wrote the following day:

> Where foxes need to be killed, let it be done by shooting. Turn-
> ing their killing into sport debases society.

The Foster bill itself did not aim to ban the killing of foxes, even
by men on horseback, *except* when it was organised for purposes
of sport. The objection, as the *Observer* pointed out, was to
"ritualisation" and to an "exclusive sport" which "commands a
key role in our culture." Macauley had commented that the old
Puritan similarly objected to bear-baiting, not on the grounds
that it gave pain to the bear, but that it gave pleasure to the
spectators. Again, Geoffrey Wheatcroft summed up the matter:

> This debate isn't an exercise in moral logic but a *Kulturkampf* in
> which hunting is a symbol (artificial as it may seem) of the old
> England which Labour's "Young Country" wants to crush and
> humiliate.[45]

The Enemy are not people with the wrong bank-balances but
people with the wrong attitude, and the policy towards them is
search-out-and-destroy. Peter Tatchell, a devotee of urine therapy
as treatment for his eczema,[46] former Labour candidate and
head of the pressure-group Outrage, who had formerly threatened to expose public figures as homosexuals, and who, on Easter
Sunday, 1998, disrupted the Archbishop of Canterbury's sermon to demand homosexual equality in the Church, was called
in to advise the Government on new punishments for "hate-
motivated" crimes. Thatchell's proposals, in the tradition of
Robespierre's Law of Prarial which dispatched those of "bad
moral character" to the guillotine, would empower judges to
impose an extra two years on prison sentences if the offender
was motivated by bigotry. (Presumably this also meant that
crimes such as armed robbery, rape, assault occasioning griev-
ous bodily harm, etc., would receive a sentencing tariff of two

years *less* if the crime in question had *not* been motivated by bigotry but had been motivated rather by simple robbery, revenge, lust or hatred on a one-on-one basis.)[47]

As 1997 and his first eight months in office drew to a close, Blair took his family on a sun-drenched holiday in the Seychelles, staying at a bungalow belonging to Albert Rene, the possibly-ex Marxist president, who had come to power by an illegal coup, made the country a one-Party dictatorship in the older sense of the term, violently destroyed political opposition, and set up a National Youth Service which called up teenagers for a year for compulsory ideological indoctrination. For an ordinary tourist to visit these islands was one thing (though some scrupulous tourists will not visit countries whose human rights records are disgusting),[48] for the Prime Minister of Great Britain to holiday there was another, and it appeared to be an eloquent comment on the Prime Minister's attitude to the institution of Parliamentary Democracy and indeed to political morality in general. It was part of Cool Britannia that the Prime Minister was not actually to be photographed being entertained by Rene or luxuriating beneath the palm-trees of paradisical tropic beaches by blue lagoons while Britain was undergoing the rigors of midwinter, as shortly before he refused to be photographed shaking hands with Gerry Adams.

In January, 1998, it was announced that the ceremonies of the Queen's State opening of Parliament would be "reformed" as they now seemed "peculiar" — the real agenda being to reduce the role of the Crown and increase that of the Prime Minister. A N Wilson commented that readers of broadsheet newspapers might have failed to notice the Queen was considering a few minor changes in Royal protocol. They included whether or not to fly the Union Jack over Buckingham Palace in the Sovereign's absence, and whether or not Princess Beatrice or the Duchess of Kent should be styled HRH. This was hardly earth-shattering news, but, Mr Wilson continued, it was the *Sun* what had the full story:

"THE PEOPLE'S MONARCHY" proclaimed the *Sun*, in what was described an "An historic Sun exclusive." Two faces stared out at us from this historic document: Her Majesty the Queen in a tiara. And the Prime Minister. Mr Blair was not in a tiara, it is true. But the iconography of the page seemed clear enough. He is stridently seen as the new Head of State.

If he is not actually replacing the present Head of State, he is hinting to her very strongly that unless she "modernises" herself, she will go the way of socialism, judge's wigs, and all the other things which get in the way of his thrusting need to make things new ...

These changes were, the *Sun* claimed, responses to "growing public dismay" and to "public outrage, led by *Sun* readers." Wilson continued:

While the *Sun*, as the most serious journal of record in Blair's Cool Britain, spelt out the heavy important constitutional implications of the "historic shake-up" at Buckingham Palace, the *Times* displayed a huge colour picture of Horse Guards Parade containing four inflatable blue drums, several times larger than Inigo Jones' building and carrying the legend "powerhouse uk". "On parade at Horse Guards", shouted the headlines, "the designer globules that will house Blair's Britain." I don't know what this means and nor, I expect, do any well-educated readers of the *Times*.[49]

In June, 1998, it was reported that the government was planning to appoint a cook to the position of Lord Lieutenant of London — Lord Lieutenant being the Queen's representative at a county level, and a position usually given to highly-distinguished service officers (the position is not a sinecure and requires real duties). Such an appointment would plainly be targeted both at traditional British culture and at any lingering doubts as to the Monarchy's dependence on the Prime Minister and the culture of New Labour. Like so many of New Labour's cultural actions, it would be not only an attack on tradition but a display of the facts of power. A public relations officer with close New Labour connections was appointed to advise the Queen.

The New Year Honours List for January, 1998, showed Blairism's ambivalent attitude to honours: the honours system was a powerful tool for social transformism but a tool of enemy origin, to be used in such a way that the use would break it. The Labour Party's richest benefactor, publisher Paul Hamlyn, was made a Peer. Mr Michael Grade, former boss of TV Channel 4 (where he earned the title of Britain's Pornographer-in-Chief from Paul Johnson after broadcasting a succession of controversial programmes), and later appointed by the Government to the team running the Millennium Dome, became a CBE. In its first months in office the Government awarded five peerages to large financial supporters, plus a knighthood to Elton John. Roger Scruton wrote in 1998:

> Harold Wilson's gesture in recommending the Beatles for the MBE was widely regarded as a tasteless innovation, an attempt to curry favour with an increasingly philistine electorate. In fact it was the first step towards what has become normal practice — the use of the honours system to reward those already rewarded by the market, while reinforcing the message that education and high culture are no longer of any special account. Pop has become the official culture of New Britain ...[50]

The political use or abuse of honours was ancient and confined to no Party in Government but this took to a new stage the process of ridiculing while using them. In obeisance to Dianamania, other honours went to the driver of the hearse at Princess Diana's funeral, the princess's senior aide and the organist who had arranged one of the funeral hymns. A knighthood and two damehoods were given to teachers who had improved a badly-performing school — doubtless worthy feats but no more than any teacher's ordinary duty.

In 1997 Squadron Leader Andy Green became the first man
to drive a car at supersonic speed. It was the sort of thing Britain
used to exult in. However on returning from his record-break-
ing run in America he received no welcome and hailed a taxi to
get home. Green's sort of achievement was not part of the spirit
of New Britain. It was the sullen nihilistic pop-singers who got
invitations to Downing Street parties, and there was an obvious
relationship here between governmental/political and general
cultural recognition. Green would receive an OBE in the New
Year Honours list, the same award given the Ceremonial Officer of the "Department of Culture" who prepared the route
for the Diana funeral. This did, however, eclipse the MBE given
to Peter Goss, the solo circumnavigator who "reversed his course
and committed himself to two days and nights of unremitting
hell" in the Southern Ocean in order to save the life of a fellow
sailor.

The *derrière-garde* Stalinist academic Eric Hobsbawm received
the high and exclusive award of Companion of Honour. His
daughter ran a public relations firm which had close ties with
the Blair government.[51] The World's leading Sovietologist and
Britain's greatest modern historian, Dr Robert Conquest, who
had done more than any other to document Stalinist genocide
and atrocities, and whose work had been more than vindicated
by the publication of formerly-secret Soviet archival material,
got nothing. A Peerage was bestowed upon Ruth Rendell, a writer
of crime stories and financial donor to the Labour Party.[52]

Meanwhile, presumably *pour encourager les autres*, Sean Connery
was denied a knighthood, allegedly on the personal intervention
of the Secretary of State for Scotland. Connery's honour was
said to have been forfeited not for any lapse in his services to
theatre but either because he had made a sexist remark or because he supported the Scottish Nationalist Party, Labour's main
rival in Scotland but otherwise a legitimate and peaceful organisation.[53] A few days later it was announced that Granada
Television's Gerry Robinson, who had been widely accused of

dumbing-down Granada in his six-year tenure (and chairman of British Sky Broadcasting), who had personally donated £10,000 to the Labour Party, would be appointed Chairman of the Arts Council, in charge of giving out government and lottery cash to cultural bodies, probably the most politico/culturally important position in the country. In June, 1998, columnist Peter McKay reported that journalist Melvin Bragg, "one of Labour's new working peers" was in line to become chairman of the new National Endowment for Science, Technology and the Arts, with a budget of up to £200 million of National Lottery money[54]. The British Council was also the subject of politically-controversial appointments.

The *Sunday Telegraph* magazine for 15 November, 1997, quoted Chris Worthy, once President of the Oxford Union and a prominent Blairite, as referring proudly to: "rock and fashion — areas in which Britain leads the world ..." Even if this were true (actually here as in practically all other such areas America leads the world), rock and fashion are not only almost totally unproductive in general or individual well-being or public wealth or goods, but are also closely connected with social alienation, drug-abuse and nihilism. Norman Lebrecht wrote:

> Pop culture has never gone short of official recognition ... What has shifted under Labour is its political credibility. Because schlock songs, grunge frocks and bare-ass movies make an awful lot of money, Tony Blair reckons they ... should be held up as shining examples to young people and invited to dinner at Downing Street — the more so when the Prime Minister's closest supporters, the Lords Levy and Puttnam, made their names in the entertainment industry.[55]

While this was true, it did not tell the full story. Schlock songs, grunge frocks and bare-ass movies were not only important as good for New Britain, but bad for the old Britain which it was both essential and satisfactory to humiliate and demoralise. Traditional light opera (mainly Gilbert & Sullivan), done for a century by the D'Oyly Carte Opera Company, was held to deserve no Arts Council money and it was reported that since its private sponsor, Sir Michael Bishop, could no longer meet the cost, the company would apparently have to close. Sir Michael was told by an Arts Council officer that: "The Arts Council wouldn't care if you disappeared off the face of the earth."[56] Major orchestras, regional theatres and other traditional cultural institutions which had depended on subsidies were in deep financial trouble.

Blair claimed that the film *The Full Monty*, a story of unemployed men in Northern England who became male strippers, reflected a new mood and celebrated "a great sense of confidence and adventure, and greater ease and comfort with ourselves". The country was discovering an "exciting" view of its future which was: "look, what we're actually good at is being inventive, creative, dynamic and outward-looking." He also claimed Britain was no longer "living in the world of a hundred years ago, when guys wore bowler hats and umbrellas, all marching down Whitehall".[57] He had previously claimed with pride if dubious accuracy that: "Our rock music is taking both America and Europe by storm."[58] Mark Steyn wrote:

> In lending his imprimatur to Cool Britannia, Mr Blair is aiding one of the most corrosive trends in Britain, the remorseless coarsening of our culture ... Every society has its dark, grunting depths: you measure yourself by how easily you can insulate yourself from them. In America and Canada, Australia and New Zealand, it's relatively easy. Only in Britain is it being trumpeted as the approved national vernacular.

> Of course, for Mr Blair's visionaries, Cool Britannia provides cultural cover for their political project — the rebranding of Britain. Most other countries have, after all, been rebranded in one fashion or another: the Soviet Union and Nazi Germany (a design logo to die for!), and, more modestly ... France, Spain, Portugal, Italy, Greece and those other European countries who

fail as nation states with such dismal regularity that they have to re-write their Constitutions every generation. Blessed are those countries whose evolution is so peaceful that their symbols and rituals come to seem quaintly incomprehensible ...[59]

Further, a new phenomena had arisen in celebrity culture. Behaviour that would have been written off as simply disgusting a few years previously now commanded lucrative interviews in the middle-market press. The obsession with public discussion of private sexual and other intimate behaviour had more behind it than titillation and pornography. It helped destroy what had been previously taken-for-granted standards of personal dignity and self-respect, part of the weakening, untying, unscrewing, the dismantling of the whole framework and structure of behaviour of the old Britain and the old world that was slated for disappearance. In June, 1998, the BBC screened its first snuff-movie, adding to its repertoire of entertainment by televising the actual death of a man with cancer.

It is hard to try to diagnose *precisely* or even define the health of a culture, since the highly visible and vocal minority who have access to the media are generally not representative of the culture as a whole, but a broad-brush picture can certainly be painted.

Footnotes

28 *Daily Mail*, 22 April 1998.
29 *Evening Standard*, 17 April 1998; *Mail on Sunday*, 19 April 1998; *Daily Mail*, 20 April 1998. This last also reported that after a BBC Radio 4 interview with Prof O'Hear the station had been inundated with calls supporting him.
30 *Daily Telegraph*, 20 April 1998.
31 *Express on Sunday*, 19 April 1998.
32 *Daily Telegraph*, 20 April 1998.

33 *Observer*, 19 April 1998.
34 *Daily Mail*, 4 May1998.
35 *Sunday Telegraph*, 17 May 1998.
36 *Daily Telegraph*, 31 January 1998.
37 *Times*, 13 January 1998.
38 *Guardian*, 13 November 1997.
39 *Daily Mail*, 28 May 1998.
40 *Sunday Telegraph*, 25 January 1998, *Mail on Sunday*, 25 January 1998.
41 *Sunday Telegraph*, 1 March 1998.
42 *Sunday Times*, 9 November 1997.
43 *Daily Telegraph* 20 January 1998.
44 See, for example, *Daily Telegraph*, 23 March 1997.
45 *Daily Telegraph* 3 March 1998.
46 "Trust me I'm a Doctor", BBC2, 20 December 1997; *Daily Telegraph*, 21 December 1997.
47 *Sunday Telegraph*, 28 December 1997.
48 A few years ago some progressive churches and Labour party figures were calling on tourists to boycott Singapore, whose regime, though authoritarian, was immeasurably more constructive and open than that of the Seychelles.
49 *Sunday Telegraph*, 8 March 1998.
50 Editorial, *The Salisbury Review*, Spring, 1998, p.41.
51 *Daily Mail*, 2 January 1998.
52 *Daily Telegraph*, 12 November 1997.
53 *Mail on Sunday*, 22 February 1998. A previous Secretary of State for Scotland, John Dalrymple of Stair, had, it is true, behaved more drastically with the politically inconvenient in 1692, arranging the mass-murder of the MacDonald sept of MacIan at Glencoe. All this, of course, sets aside the intriguing question of why Connery would *want* an honour from a Great Britain he wished to break up.
54 *Daily Mail*, 22 June 1998.
55 *Daily Telegraph*, 1 April 1998.

56 *Daily Mail,* 26 February 1998.
57 *Daily Telegraph,* 22 December 1997; 24 December 1997.
58 *Guardian,* 22 July 1997.
59 *Sunday Telegraph,* 28 December 1997.

Chapter 3 History and All That

It was said that in the dying years of the Roman Empire an over-bold Emperor, the Immortal Valerian, was captured by the Persians. He was not killed outright but was used in the Persian Court as a foot-stool and mounting-block, and when he finally died was stuffed and hung swinging from the rafters as a sign to all of how the equations of power now stood.

This is a neat illustration of the role New Labour sees for Britain's History, traditions and, ultimately, its National Identity. One goal of *Kulturkampf* is the creation of a culture in which dissent is impossible to express. In New Britain terms this means a state in which cultural conservatives have nothing to say and no means of saying it. In this it resembles George Orwell's Newspeak, language designed to make political dissent impossible to express and practically impossible to conceive of. Thus, in a future Britain where popular culture is dominated by rock-music, the *Sun*, Coronation Street, the World Cup, the creators of the Sensations exhibition, the *Guardian*, Terence Conran, Alexander McQueen, Oprah Winfrey, post-modernist deconstructionism and the legacies of Guido Versace and Princess Diana, the culture of old Britain would hardly be able even to set up an alternative.

Constant iconoclastic social change tends to reduce conservatives to cultural pessimism and despair and — this is by no means the least satisfactory bonus for the Elect of the *Zeitgeist* — to deep personal unhappiness. These things also reduce conservatives' political effectiveness. If the elderly Polish lady who had escaped from Stalinist Russia, now living on a pension in a small apartment with a picture of the Pope on the wall, could be driven into covering her face in her hands with the words: "it's all so horrible!", if the old soldier once a pillar of the local British Legion or Conservative Club could no longer muster the spirit to defend the Royal Family after reading the latest interview with the Duchess of York, if the school or university student was told with a thousand voices that dignity, courage, chastity, honour were not so much out-dated as irrelevant, that was all victory. Coarsening and lowering of culture is a strategy to implement a final solution for cultural conservatism.

It is important that whatever is familiar and loved by conservatives be attacked and destroyed, if not by government and politicians as such, then by the cultural Nomenklatura in a tacit and perhaps "deniable" alliance with the government. The projected end of the last cultural conservative might be something like that of the last Neanderthal in William Golding's *The Inheritors*, who dies of grief, huddled weeping against the cave-rock that marks the burial-place of his old chief, after the "New People" have obliterated his society.

The lifestyle-obsessed rich and bourgeoisie are relatively little problem, or at most a problem of a different kind. The military traditions and values can be seen as probably doomed when Britain appears to have no independent military future and in any case are being remorselessly assaulted by political correctness, but it remains imperative that culturally conservative traditions and values be eliminated.

Respect for the Monarchy may be seen as a last redoubt of cultural conservatism, either its Alamo or its Rorke's Drift, and the Monarchy is of little *long-term* value to New Labour (besides, some future Monarch might more be assertive than the present one). However, as Blair's behaviour at the Diana funeral and at the Queen's 50th wedding anniversary showed, a cowed Monarchy which exists as a PR agency for New Labour is very useful not only for corralling loyalty but also for dismaying, demoralising and discrediting cultural conservatism. It is important that enemy morale be crushed on a permanent, institutionalised basis, its values seem to be dead, silent, motionless and impotent as "the stuffed thing that hung in the Persian court".[60] Much of traditional British life must be reduced, perhaps with tears and plentiful use of the word "nostalgia", to History, embalmed, a museum or theme park.

Enoch Powell had once described how he formed a certain idea of England. It had been in English churches:

> ... Beneath the tall tracery of a perpendicular East window and the coffered ceiling of the chantry chapel. From brass and stone, from line and effigy, their eyes looked out at us, and we gazed into them, as if we would win some answer from their silence. Tell us what it is that binds us together; show us the clue that leads through a thousand years; whisper to us the secret of this charmed life of England, that we in our time may know how to hold it fast ...[61]

With innumerable other writers, some other Conservative politicians had also tried to capture the essence of Britain by an evocation of the country, however gropingly. Stanley Baldwin spoke, rather strangely, in 1924 of:

> The sounds of England, the tinkle of the hammer on the anvil in the country smithy, the corncrake on a dewy morning, the sound of the scythe against the whetstone, the sight of a plough-team coming over a hill, the sight that has been in England since England was a land, and may be seen in England long after the Empire has perished and every works in England has ceased to function, for centuries the one eternal sight of England.[62]

John Major, though doing little to encourage any sort of conservative cultural fight-back, and apparently hardly aware of the cultural war that was helping destroy his administration, borrowed from Orwell to evoke:

Long shadows on country grounds, warm beer, invincible green
suburbs and old maids cycling to holy communion through the
morning mist.[63]

A Cool Britannia whose salient points of existence are rock-
musicians, fashion-designers, millionaire soccer club managers
and recipients of prolefeed who feel the events of Coronation
Street more deeply than those of the actual world is simply in-
compatible with a Britain whose history is a living culture — the
Britain that is a part and product of (to make a very small and
idiosyncratic list) Alfred the Great, Mallory, Purcell, Shakespeare,
Dr Johnson, Nelson, Turner, Wellington, Constable, Sir Walter
Scott, *Rewards and Fairies*, Ralph Vaughan Williams, Robert Louis
Stevenson, Gainsborough, Gilbert & Sullivan, *The Ballad of the
White Horse*, John Buchan, Arthur Ransome, Richmal Crompton,
"BB", *The Wind in the Willows*, "Bartimeus", W E Johns, J R R
Tolkien, C. S. Forester, Douglas Bader, Trooping the Colour,
Meccano, John Wyndham, Hornby trains, Sir Frank Whittle,
Ernest Bevin, C S Lewis, Geoffrey Household, Berkeley Mather,
Rosemary Sutcliff, Dr Who, Kenneth More in *North West Fron-
tier*, Colonel Wintle, *Carry On* films, Lord Denning, *Genevieve*, vil-
lage cricket, Dan Dare, Benny Hill, Hugh Gaitskell, Alec
Guinness, *Dad's Army*, Thomas the Tank Engine, and, late and
perhaps closing the circle, John Boorman's 1981 film *Excalibur*
(this last a smashing riposte to the notion that satires like *Monty
Python and the Holy Grail* had succeeded in killing the deep cultural resonance and magic of the Arthurian myth). I do not
suggest the names on this second list add up to a cultural unity
but what they do have in common is congruence with various
aspects of the mainstream of Britain's traditional culture. The
two are as incompatible as the Soviet Union and the writings of
Solzhentisyn: they cannot ultimately both exist in the same culture and one or the other has to go.

Thus while Blair himself has shown little or no interest in
history, history has emerged as one of Blairism's principal targets.

The British culture has been steeped in and dependent upon history to a quite extraordinary degree, and a national change in consciousness cannot take place until attitudes to British history have been revolutionised. Historic heroes and great achievements must be "debunked" and satirised and occasions of historic guilt and shame accentuated or invented.

This is partly governmental, partly the occupation of the Nomenklatura and chattering classes. A thousand small battles are being fought up and down the land, in schools, in Universities, in displays and labelling of museum exhibits. Despite representations, the Government refused to issue a stamp to commemorate the 50th anniversary of the Berlin Airlift, in which 43 British airmen died, though the German, US and French Governments honoured the occasion.[64] Similarly, the Government refused to fund the building of a memorial to British servicemen who died in Japanese captivity in World War II, claiming the cost of memorials was met from private donations. This would be unexceptional except for the fact that the day before the refusal the Prime Minister announced a large government contribution to a memorial to victims of the Irish potato famine of the Nineteenth Century, the most powerful icon of anti-British sentiment and political rhetoric in Irish America.[65] The 80th anniversary of the Royal Air Force passed without official mention in 1998, but the BBC did, on 7 April, screen a documentary arguing that, contrary to "popular legend" the RAF had not saved Britain from invasion in the Battle of Britain[66]. In conformity with the *Zeitgeist*, the Union Jack insignia was removed from the tail-fins of British Airways aircraft and replaced with a variety of multicultural designs at some cost to safety in air-traffic control. Money for the preservation of all manner of ancient and beautiful buildings, even, it appeared, the Bodleian Library,[67] was unavailable, though there were grants for all manner of rubbish-art. Money was given for one artist to make a full-sized replica steam-locomotives in brick, but not to save real and historic steam-locomotives from the scrap-yard cutting torch. The Master of the Queen's Music asked for a reworked National Anthem for a "new age", possibly borrowing from Mao Tse-Tung to claim that "the vitality of state and social institutions depends upon perpetual renewal."[68]

These, and innumerable other such items, are small things on their own, but it is the cumulative effect that matters. Science-fiction writer Poul Anderson has a vivid description of a relentless, ceaseless propaganda bombardment:

> The music was so amplified as to be audible to the very out-skirts of town. And it never ended. This was a perpetual choir. Priests, acolytes, pilgrims, were always on hand to step in when any of the six hundred and one wearied. I failed to imagine how it must be to live in that day-and-night haze of canticle. If you were dweller in Siloam ... you'd soon stop noticing on a conscious level. But wouldn't the sound weave into your thoughts, dreams, bones, finally into your soul?[69]

It is instructive to look, by way of example, at what happened in the early months of Blairism to the heritage of the Royal Navy, historically and to a quite unique degree one of Britain's most important social and cultural institutions as well as a Defence force.

By no coincidence the government had Admiralty Arch, the Navy's historic headquarters in London, and until recently the home of Britain's senior serving Naval officer, turned into a refuge for the homeless when there were thousands of other empty buildings in the Metropolis more suitable. A politician posed there with the homeless for a one-off (for them) fried breakfast. The First Sea Lord, the professional head of the Navy, was pushed out of Admiralty House into a small flat in Kensington to make way for a Labour Politician, Margaret Beckett, the President of the Board of Trade, who claimed she needed a larger and more prestigious place to entertain. The Greenwich Royal Naval College, built by Sir Christopher Wren and one of the most beautiful groups of buildings in the world, listed as a World Heritage site, was also listed to be vacated by the Navy late in 1998. By the beginning of 1998 the government had shown no interest in its future, though spending in the vicinity of three-quarters of a billion pounds on the Millennium Dome nearby.

Government funds for preserving historic monuments were targeted away from this kind of history. As far as the Government had anything to do with it, icons of Britain's naval and whole maritime heritage and traditions seemed to be literally for the scrap-heap. Famous ships from World War II appeared doomed, such as Britain's last destroyer from that war, HMS *Cavalier*. A plan to restore the last motor mine-sweeper of World War II, rotting in Stoke Creek, was abandoned for lack of funds, and a spokesman for the trust attempting to raise funding said the vessel might have to be broken up[70].

A paddle steamer, the *Medway Queen*, one of the most famous vessels from Dunkirk, where it was said to have rescued 7,000 men and was one of the last away, its crew still picking swimming soldiers from the sea after the breakwater was in German hands, sank at its moorings after the trust attempting to save it was refused lottery cash. Mrs Noreen Chambers, secretary of the trust, said: "To let her go after all this time would be a disgrace. It would be an insult to out nautical history and a slap in the face to all who were so gallant at Dunkirk."[71]

Britain's first submarine, the *Resurgam*, which had sunk off north Wales in 1880, was discovered on the sea bottom in 1997, but no money was made available to preserve it.[72] It was being gradually broken up by the sea, and could have been raised and preserved for an estimated £1,000,000. While this money was not available, £220,000 of lottery money was granted to provide snout-operated showers, porcine toys and under-floor heating in pigsties at an educational farm centre at Sellafield.[73] Even the continuing restoration and preservation of the SS *Great Britain*, one of the most historically significant steamships in the world from an engineering point of view, and a major tourist attraction for a depressed part of Bristol (a city with major unemployment-related problems), seemed in the balance in 1998.

Meanwhile the Lord Chancellor, Lord Irvine, had £650,000 spent on refurbishing his official residence, including £56,000 on hand-printed wall-paper, as well as a £3,000 on a pedestal lavatory surrounded by Pugin-style panelling and specially adapted to function like a Victorian water-closet.[74] After being widely criticised for this expenditure he was reported to have hired a second aide at a salary of £60,000 to restore his public image.[75]

It was announced that Navy uniforms would be changed to allow Moslem women serving in the Navy to wear veils over their faces although in Islamic countries like Turkey and Pakistan female naval personnel do not wear veils.[76] Meanwhile, the Navy itself was besieged by an apparently endless series of sex scandals, families being broken up and careers ruined as a result of maintaining the politically-correct *diktat* that women serve at sea in warships. The enemy targeted by these policies was not a foreign invasion fleet but the existing Naval ethos and its associated traditions. Meanwhile, in further obeisance to political correctness, Britain's latest submarines would also require lavatories even more expensive than Lord Irvine's and, presumably, extra pipes and vulnerable skin-fittings for their mixed-sex crews.

The British pavilion at the Lisbon Expo was revealingly described in July, 1998, by *Daily Mail* writer Ross Benson. "Oceans" was the theme of the whole Expo, and, Benson said, in the crosscurrents of history no nation had made a more profound impact on the high seas than Britain. This should have been a glorious chance to show to the 12 million people who would visit what Britain could do. There was, however, practically nothing about Britain's sea-faring traditions or heritage or indeed anything of interest. Practically no-one was visiting the British exhibition, though other nations' exhibitions had long queues for admittance.

The British exhibition started with a T-shirt pinned to the wall bearing the inquiry: "Britain: What springs to mind now?"

It was, Benson said, a question which had clearly defeated HPICM, the "creative consultancy" which designed it and which was charged with doing the Body Zone in the Greenwich Dome.

A moving walkway went through an electric blue darkness to some model umbrellas which popped up and down in front of a video of people dancing and eating. The next chamber contained peep-holes which revealed slogans proclaiming Britain's commitment to keeping the seas clear of pollution. It concluded with the story-board of a ship which had made one voyage to Lisbon before foundering in 1690.

And that, to all intents, is the sum of it ... But whereas we have chosen to ignore the likes of Drake and Raleigh and Captain Cook, the Spanish have put together an eight-minute planetarium-style display dedicated to their explorers and navigators. "We are proud of our heritage," the Spanish official explained.[77]

In April, 1998, it was announced that the Army would be rebranded with a more caring image after "private research" had found that its discipline was seen as repressive and robotic, and Army life and culture to be time-warped, low-tech, old-fashioned, rigid and class-based. The report was based on a survey of 300 civilians and "opinion leaders", and even the consultants who wrote the report described these views as "impoverished and stereotyped."[78] To create a more multi-racial Army the Government published a patronising parody of Lord Kitchener's famous World War I recruiting poster: "Your Country Needs You" with the Field Marshal's face replaced by a black soldier like something from *The Black and White Minstrel Show*.[79] The Army had already bent to political correctness by adopting such progressive measures as "gender neutral" physical standards, meaning male soldiers' strength standards were reduced so females did not feel inferior in this respect. This was in spite of the fact that in battle lives and victory might depend on the ability of soldiers to carry ammunition or operate heavy weapons and equipment by muscle-power, quite apart from all the well-documented problems of discipline associated with having women serve beside men. The Israeli Army, with crucial man-power problems, had had women serve in front-line units briefly, and found the experiment a complete failure. The armed forces also had to train female jet-fighter pilots, millions of pounds' worth of training being thrown away if they became pregnant.

*   *   *

Britain's military traditions are only a small part of its national identity: by Continental standards Britain has never been a very militarised society. They are, however, a part which it is worth considering here as a pointer to what is happening in the whole culture.

There are, in Britain, a number of military museums: not only the great ones like the Imperial War Museum, the National Army Museum and Edinburgh Castle, but, throughout the land, a number associated with historic local regiments. One such is the Regiments of Gloucestershire Museum located at the old Gloucester docks, an area which also has refurbished historic warehouses and moorings for some antique ships and boats.

The Regiments of Gloucestershire museum I select here by way of one example among many others. There are depictions of the battle fought near Alexandria in 1801, when two lines of soldiers, surrounded, fought back-to-back, earning the regiment the distinction of wearing a badge on the back as well as the front of the head-gear, a reproduction of one of the two private soldiers who carried the Colours in the last charge at the Battle of Salamanca when six relays of officers and sergeants had been killed carrying them previously, and the toast drunk in the Officer's Mess following a battle in 1811 when Mr Vice, instead of moving the normal toast of "Gentlemen, the King!", moved "The King, Mr President!" because Mr Vice and Mr President were the only two officers left. There are dioramas of heroic deeds in World War I and World War II, a photograph of a Regimental children's fancy-dress party in Malta between the wars, displays of crosses and badges carved by Gloucester POWs in torture-camps during the Korean War, a mess port-warmer still used on special occasions, and much more.

These military museums remind one of how richly this culture interacted with the traditions, values, and lives of the nation. A great part of the displays are homely, individual, celebrating, like the toast at Bares, some sort of *personal* behaviour. Britain's army, compared to those of Continental Europe, was generally small. Even in the First World War conscription was not introduced until 1916. Nonetheless, the military culture was there in the background. The aristocracy were expected to provide a part of the Officer class at least disproportionate to their numbers, and in village and suburban life the retired officer — "The Major", "The Colonel" — was a respected and leading figure in the district. The Army, like the Navy, was not only responsible for the physical defence of the Nation, it was also a guardian of values. Officers were expected to conduct themselves well and set an example in society at large, even in matters such as religious observance. So, increasingly, were the Men, whose image following the Crimean War gradually changed from that of dangerous brutes to heroes. Quite apart from warlike considerations, the Army, like the Navy, provided a kind of background cultural richness — even of splendour — as well as a feeling of National unity and National identity.

The second impression such a museum creates today is of the futility of all the heroism, and the *lostness* of all the tradition and values. The causes and values have become irrelevant, the frame of reference has been removed. If Britain is to be subsumed into Europe now, why did it fight and bleed to preserve its independence from Napoleon? Why did those two surviving officers toast the King when 180 years later (when there were men alive whose fathers had been born when there were men still living who remembered Napoleon) the British media could pour every kind of insult on the Queen without protest? If that toast was "God bless the King", what King? For that matter,

what God? Why didn't the *Birkenhead* men rush the life-boats
and save themselves from the sharks? Why the suffering of the
First World War, if at the end Britain is to be a second-rate prov-
ince of a German-dominated Europe anyway? Why did those
regiments bother policing an Empire? Or defending South Ko-
rea?

*   *   *

At one level, the Blair regime is promising a new, cool, Britannia with a repackaged national identity. On the other, it seems
the whole thing is finished — national identity, sovereignty, history, the works. Britain's cultural Nomenklatura has become
schizophrenic.

It appears that Britain as a full member of the European
Union will be committed to a single European foreign policy
and defence policy, and to a common European citizenship with
rights and obligations to be defined by European courts. The
agreed single currency will be managed by a European central
bank, in Frankfurt, which will control the gold and dollar reserves of all member countries, and interest rates. The former
heads of national banks will be reduced toregional spokesmen.
Obviously a common currency will need common economic
and political institutions.

This, even without other binding treaties, would of itself be
enough to hamstring national sovereignty. It is obvious that a
country which loses control of its economy loses its independence. A Britain without its own money could not finance independent foreign or defence policies, let alone a war even on the
limited scale of the Falklands War if its territory was attacked.
Independent armed forces and existence as an independent nation can be expected to move gradually out of the question.

At the end of New Labour's first year in government the
abdication of sovereignty was already advanced, though little
reported except through the efforts of Christopher Booker and

a few others (the process had of course begun much earlier). In 1997 it was reported that the European Commission's London office was already giving out regional booklets describing each of the different "regions" of Britain — "Scotland", "The South East" etc — as "a region of the European Union" with no mention of England, the United Kingdom or Great Britain. East Sussex, for example, had ceased to be an English county and had become part of Interreg II, along with a large part of upper Normandy. Each region, it was said, would send two unelected members to the committee of Regions in Brussels, and the existing local councils would gradually disappear.[80]

These developments may be viewed as good or bad things. It is indisputable that they are important. However few in Britain — at least in England — seemed to realise how much was at stake. The way the European Union has evolved has made the process additionally confusing. It was not, for example, foreseen when the EEC was being set up that Germany would be reunited and become the dominant power in the union. It is another issue that, given EEC integration, Scotland will have little obvious reason to remain in the union with Britain at all.

Perhaps, however, it was not a question of public ignorance but public impotence — in terms of public-choice theory, very few pressure-groups in this context have the lobbying-power to do anything. Here public-bar opinion cut little ice.

It was another issue again that the attack on almost every kind of traditional institution was increasingly leaving Britain without a focus of National identity — even football, one of the few major institutions in a flourishing condition, could be a focus of and force for divisiveness rather than unity. Nationalist and separatist issues dominated Scottish media and public discourse and the end of the Union had moved with surprising swiftness out of the realm of the unthinkable.

There was also a backlash of English chauvinism. Suddenly there are more *English* flags — St George's crosses, not Union Jacks — on car-stickers as well as at football matches, especially near the border. This was a long way from the accomplished break-up of the United Kingdom but the social and cultural groundwork for a break was being laid. Columnist Simon Heffer wrote as St. George's Day, 1998 approached:

> The other evening, walking in the dusk past the Palace of Westminster, I glanced skywards. The Union Jack was being hauled down from over the houses of Parliament; and the sight prompted in me a mixture of anger and discomfort ... We shall not be happy until the old flag is run down for the last time, and the simple banner of St. George flies over the Palace of Westminster.[81]

A very few years previously such a thing could hardly have been written without being dismissed as the ramblings of a political crank, wedded to a hopeless cause so *outré* as to be comic to anyone else, like the girl driven mad by too much study for her Edinburgh exams giving out Scots Nationalist and pro-Hitler leaflets to bemused wartime commandos in the Hebrides in Evelyn Waugh's *Sword of Honour*.

Given the apparently imminent break-up of the union and the submergence of Britain in Europe, why was the government trying with such intensity to reshape national identity and consciousness? Given the way things were going, it looked as if there was not going to *be* a national identity much longer. Why bother with expensive, complex and potentially hazardous devolution measures for Scotland, Wales and Northern Ireland when their future was not going to be decided in the British Isles?

Such questions tend to have complex answers: politicians to some extent live for the exercise of power and a place in the history books. Part of the answer may be that Britain, without the Cold War, the Empire or the sustaining memory of the heroisms of World War II had, for the first time in centuries, no national or unifying purpose and nothing important to do. Better, perhaps, to be remembered for abolishing ancient traditions and values than not be remembered at all. Partly, of course, those shaping events may not know what they are doing and are not fully in control of the process or logic of developments.

Part of the answer may be that the government is trying to reshape the national identity and consciousness not in spite of the coming European union but because of it. A Britain whose historic culture has been destroyed may not find the loss of sovereignty such a great matter.

* * *

In December, 1997, the Royal Yacht *Britannia* paid off. It was not to be replaced (the cost of a replacement would have been less than that of one modern fighter aircraft or of the reported planned refit of a submarine due for scrapping), though even Spain has a Royal Yacht and many other smaller and poorer countries have vessels that fulfil its diplomatic, trade, flag-showing and other functions. Argentina, for example, had a tradition of splendid-looking sailing ships, such as the *Presidente Samiento* and the *Libertad*, which had both training and ambassadorial roles. This struck at two traditional British institutions, the Royal Navy and the Royal Family. The *Sun* commented on the Royal Family's discomfiture at the *Britannia's* decommissioning:

> She was also dubbed the Love Boat after four royal couples went on honeymoon on [*sic*] *Britannia*. But all four marriages — Princess Margaret and Lord Snowdon, Princess Ann and Mark Phillips, Prince Charles and Diana, and Prince Andrew and Fergie — ended in divorce.

The *Sun* also carried five large colour pictures of the Queen in tears at the decommissioning ceremony, and editorialised:

> Sad farewells. First the train went, now the yacht. Little by little, the royals are seeing how the other half has to live. It was

touching to see the Queen shed a tear over Britannia. Was her
emotion because she is becoming a more down-to-earth monarch ... or was she upset at seeing another perk bite the dust?

Auberon Waugh remarked:

Here is the real voice of modern Britain in all its odiousness.[82]

The reference to the Royal train had a certain piquancy. By
May, 1998, it was being used by Mrs Blair, though another private citizen, inspired by her example to try to hire it, was unsuc-
cessful in this endeavour.

After pushing through the Scots devolution referendum, the
Prime Minister banned as outmoded tartans, bagpipes and other
traditional symbols of Scotland's heritage[83] from the 1997 Commonwealth Heads of Government Meeting in Edinburgh. Instead, the visiting dignitaries representing 51 Commonwealth
countries were treated to a video, "Britain, the young country".
The Prime Minister announced again that: "There is a new
British identity."

It was easy to dismiss this as meaningless noise like Harold
Wilson's White Heat of the Technological Revolution (in 1964
Wilson had campaigned under the slogan "Let's go with Labour for the New Britain"). However Blair actually meant it. It
was part of the obsessive attack on the iconography of British
History. Writer and Conservative candidate Boris Johnson described this video as:

Stunning images of the best of British, brash young designers,
advertising whizkids, hot young chefs from Sir Terence Conran's
Mezzo restaurant, cool young Liam and Noel in their Kangol
finery, and of course, the Dear Leader himself ...

Blair's vision of Britain, he continued, was:

Lots of young designers specialising in buttock exposure, a few

loutish and derivative Britpopstars, multi-millionaire restaura-
teurs who charge you £5 for a bun. It catches the taste of the
moment, all right.[84]

In fact, "Britpop" had little British about it: it was basically a
clone of American underculture with added Nihilism. It had
the politico/cultural purpose of dissolving and destroying the
institutions of conservative cultural norms. It was also valuable
as a sort of cultural terror-weapon.

It was significant that Blair's patronage should have been
publicly extended to Oasis, one of the most aggressive and Nihilistic rock-bands. As Orwell said of the goose-step, it was something ludicrous in other circumstances used to demonstrate crude
power to dismay and demoralise opposition: "We have won,
and you daren't laugh at us. It is ugly and you daren't laugh.
Your world has ended."

It heralded a world where traditional notions of beauty would
have no place, partly through indifference to them but also because they were identified as the doomed culture of conservatism. Beautiful new works of art or evocations of nobility were in
New Labour's Britain notable by their virtually total absence,
as the entries for the strangely-named Turner Prize demonstrated. The government announced the appointment of a committee of celebrities, politicians and business people, under the
chairman of Foreign Office Minister Derek Fatchett, to pro-
mote the image of Cool Britannia to the world. These included
Stella McCartney, daughter of Sir Paul, Mr Peter Mandelson,[85]
and Judy Simpson, "Nightshade" in the television Gladiator
show.[86] Members would advise the government on "style" issues, including diplomatic protocol. Mr Blair informed the press
that:

We are modern Britain, we are young and effective, we've got
to challenge the image that Britain is traditionally based in aspects like Buckingham Palace but also in the traditional old
smokestack industries.[87]

Simon Brocklebank-Fowler, a former Tory candidate, writing in *The Spectator* that the Conservative Party must be "cooler" in order to appease "the people who make the nation's cultural weather", argued that William Hague was: "the best looker in the Conservative leadership race ... a good enough reason for him to get the job in the age of television, even without his other merits." This might be paraphrased as: "Resistance is useless."

Footnotes

60 Evelyn Waugh, *Helena* (Penguin, UK, 1981) p.70

61 Quoted by Peregrine Worsthorne, *Daily Telegraph*, 23 February, 1998

62 Quoted by Boris Johnson, *Daily Telegraph*, 22 October 1997

63 *ibid*

64 *Daily Mail*, 25 March 1998

65 *Daily Mail*, 21 November 1997

66 It is trite knowledge that the Germans did not have the resources to mount a D-Day style invasion of Britain in 1940 - the Royal Navy was several times the size of the *Kriegsmarine* — but had they established air superiority, destroyed the RAF and been able to carry out unopposed bombing of docks, naval bases, factories, cities, etc. the war might well have been lost anyway. The claim that the battle saved Britain is as certain as anything can be in war and there seems no valid reason to dispute it or attack and "debunk" what is basically a straw man apart from a further discrediting of what are seen as conventional mythologies. At about the same time the BBC was running a series of advertisements mocking and ridiculing the patriotic wartime naval film *In Which We Serve*.

67 *Daily Telegraph*, 15 November 1997

68 *Daily Mail*, 15 June 1998

69 Poul Anderson, *Operation Chaos* (Severn House, Surrey, 1995), p.182

70 *Navy News*, January 1998

71 *Daily Mail,* 2 January 1998

72 *Daily Telegraph,* 22 February 1998

73 *Daily Telegraph,* 27 March 1998

74 *Daily Telegraph,* 24 February 1998

75 *Daily Telegraph,* 7 April 1998

76 *Daily Mail,* 7 January 1998 ; 8 Jan 1998. It is sometimes forgotten that the Royal Navy is in one aspect a specifically Christian institution: the blessing of God has traditionally been invoked for ships at launching and ships' companies have regular prayers and Divine Services, taken by the Captain when there is no chaplain. "Fear God Honour the King." is a Naval motto.

77 *Daily Mail,* 4 July 1998

78 *Daily Telegraph,* 12 April 1998

79 Lord Kitchener, incidentally, was also the subject of a "debunking" by the BBC in 1998. Previous programmes had "debunked" legless air ace Douglas Bader and depicted Boy Scout founder General Robert Baden Powell as a suspected paedophile. The BBC programme portrayed him as a homosexual, sadist, war criminal and military incompetent.

80 *Daily Telegraph,* 27 December 1997

81 *Daily Mail,* 20 April 1998

82 *Daily Telegraph,* 15 December 1997

83 It might be objected that these things were relatively recent and to some extent manufactured. They were, however, at least as much part of a living culture as was some pageantry of more unbrokenly ancient lineage.

84 *Daily Telegraph,* 22 October 1997

85 *Daily Telegraph,* 28 March 1998

86 *Daily Mail,* 31 March 1998

87 *Daily Telegraph,* 28 March 1998. "Smokestack industries" presumably included things like heavy engineering and shipbuilding.

Chapter 4 Domed Down

Some conservatives, contemplating British culture today, may find reassurance in the adage that there is nothing new under the sun, and in the observation that many present social phenomena have been seen before. It is mere doomsaying, sensationalism, or indulgence in cultural combat and controversy for its own sake, according to this wisdom, to see some fundamental threat or collapse in changes in things as ephemeral as fashions, books, films, speech-patterns, educational, sexual and penal theories, the ethos of the armed forces or the Party in Government. We have been there before and survived.

If teenage thugs and gangs mug and terrorise law-abiding citizens, it might be said, they are hardly worse than the often psychopathic members of the Hellfire Club had once been; the Royal Family has been involved in scandal often in British history: the Prince Regent was more savagely attacked and lampooned in the newspapers of the day than was the Prince of Wales in 1997 — even Queen Victoria had been widely attacked at times during her reign; the great British institutions of Parliament and Ministers and Church had often been in disrepute; if the House of Lords was under pressure, Gilbert and Sullivan had been ridiculing it in *Iolanthe* more than a hundred years before.

If art, music, literature and fashion seemed degraded and ugly, was not this simply the way innovation in art always appeared at first? Turner, Tchaikovsky and T S Eliot had been radical once. Widespread illiteracy is not new — it was common before the 1870 *Education Act.* If there was rubbishy journalism, pseudo-art and cults of mindless sports, hadn't there always been? The proletarianisation of culture has been a complaint — as Professor John Carey documented in *The Intellectuals and the Masses* — of some of the nastiest snobs and socio/political bullies who considered the pleasures and tastes of the general public unbearable.

Wasn't the besetting temptation for cultural conservatives to look at the past through rose-tinted glasses and dream nostalgically of a "Golden Age" which had never actually existed? Furthermore, is not dwelling on the past a psychological phenomenon closely connected with neurosis?

Many of the rituals, ceremonies and pageantry which seemed to define "Old Britain" were in fact of recent origin or had been changed many times. And if the *Medway Queen* was allowed to sink at its moorings, the *Golden Hind* was allowed to disintegrate and eventually be built over at Deptford Dockyard despite Queen Elizabeth's wish that it be preserved forever (the remains may be under the dockyard yet). The ugliness of industrialisation spoiling the countryside had been lamented by Dickens and Blake.[88] Religious certainties seemed under attack, but Darwin had rocked them in the Nineteenth Century. Churches might be almost empty and racked with struggles over the truth of the Resurrection and sexual preferences, but there had been crises in the church before. The preceding two hundred years had been full of changes and the "moral essence" of Britain had survived them.

It might be perhaps a comforting thought that the more things changed the more they were the same. If the Royal Navy of the late 1990s had a series of sex-scandals as a result of women serving at sea, women had been at sea in British warships before. Sailor's wives may have helped serve guns at Trafalgar. Nelson himself had scandalised many by his affair with Lady Hamilton, but the Nelsonian Navy had been anything but decadent — it had won glorious victories and founded the greatest

Naval traditions.

Unfortunately for such cultural conservatives, phrases such as "the more things change the more they are the same" are, outside a limited context, meaningless. Looking to the past may have more than mere neurosis to it: the White Rose in Nazi Germany or the works of Solzhenitsyn were not products of the *Zeitgeist.*

What is now being seen is not the normal ebb and flow of change as some conservatives may see in an organic society all the time, but an attack on the moral essence, combined with what looks like a general dissolution of those social and cultural structures which provide that moral essence with both definition and means of existence. There has probably never since the Dark Ages been a situation in Britain where change was so accompanied by the apparent shattering of *all* certainties — not merely of moral certainties but also of faith in that whole structure or way (The *Tao*, as C. S. Lewis put in *The Abolition of Man*) which makes existence viable.

Further, aspects of the present intellectual *regression* seem almost unprecedented in modern times. In the 1950s a bright and ambitious young man might typically want to be an aircraft designer, and the culture of the day would have reinforced this. In Cool Britannia the equivalent career would probably be as a football or rock-star. The Minister with Responsibility for Science, Margaret Beckett, was reported to have told the Lords Select Committee on Science and Technology in November, 1997, that perceptions of science careers among young people were "most alarming" and "deeply depressing".[89] If illiteracy had been widespread in the Nineteenth Century, it also had been tending to diminish, not increase.

Nihilism has not previously enjoyed the obvious patronage of both the Nomenklatura and officialdom to anything like the degree it does today. It is a fact that though the paintings of Turner when first exhibited were seen as breaking some of the established rules of art, they did *not* do violence to certain permanent and enduring values as the "Sensations" exhibition, for example, *tried* to. Mozart did *not* violate or try to violate the rules of musical beauty as rock-music does. Never before has someone like Francis Bacon, whose credo was summed up in the words: "Man now realises that he is an accident, that he is a completely futile being, that he has to play out the game without reason ..." been taken as a cultural Oracle. William Blake, himself one of the most radical and innovative of artists, wrote the striking protest:

> Degrade first the arts if you'd Mankind degrade,
> Hire idiots to paint with cold and hot shade.
> Give high praise to the worst, leave the best in disgrace,
> *And with the labours of ignorance fill every place.*

Further, at least since the Enlightenment — some might say at least since The Sermon on the Mount — the human race has had at least a dim and flickering idea of *spiritual* progress, in more recent times in association with ideas of intellectual, scientific and material progress. This may be seen even in some ancient Greek and Roman writers.

What one has seen until recently, certainly in the last two hundred years, has been unsteady and irregular, but real, progress in civic behaviour and in general education. "Dumbing down" — a term which significantly was unknown until a couple of years ago — now seems to be affecting many parts of life. A visit to a newspaper library and a comparison of today's newspapers with those of even ten, let alone twenty-five, years ago seems to provide further evidence of this, and a comparison of men's and women's general-interest magazines does so even more eloquently. *Blackwoods* and *Encounter* are gone (*Argosy* went before them). Although there are a number of good British and American specialist magazines on subjects like history and astronomy, an overwhelming impression of the contents of newsagents' shelves are of fashion, infantile quasi-pornography and occultism. Dumbing down is not only useful for destroying cultural opposition. Religion failed to fulfil Marx's description as an Opium of the People, but soccer, sex, and scandals (preferably Royal) provide very acceptable substitutes. They are particularly effective when in the so-called general interest area there is in effect *no choice* or alternative to a pervasive trash-culture.

While "Men's magazines" like *Loaded* are significant here as indicators of the state of popular culture, women's magazines are perhaps a more significant case in point. For an intelligent young woman growing up in Britain today, there is hardly a single women's magazine available not obsessed with sex, sleaze, titillation, a junk-celebrity culture and the most shallow and vacuous kind of vanity, frequently, as with the tabloid press, involving the most vicious violations of individuals' privacy (One exception has been *The Lady*. It is ironic that a magazine so titled comes closest to the idea of an intelligent feminist of yore of what an intelligent women's magazine might be like. Another exception is *The People's Friend*, a highly unprogressive, indeed old-fashioned paper which published light romances along with household material). It was with amazement that I came across, in a doctor's waiting-room, one glossy women's magazine which carried, utterly untypically, a feature on the breeding habits of Antarctic penguins. I wondered if the editor who commissioned it kept her job.

When the tone and content of these women's magazines were questioned, their defenders generally claimed they were harmless fantasy. The fact that they had become almost all that was available was glossed over. This was a long way from the story of "Sarah and the Seaplane" — the story of an independent-minded girl who wanted to be an aircraft pilot — which pioneering feminist Betty Friedan pointed to in *The Feminine Mystique* as an example of how magazine stories might enlarge young women's horizons. It is much easier to rebrand a culture regressing into infantility.

Peter Mandelson claimed:

We have world-class design companies. We are not just the country of warm beer. We are the country of John Galliano, Alexander McQueen and Stella McCartney.[90]

It might have been thought that these exemplars were industrial, aerospace or computer designers. In fact they were fashion designers. Galliano and McQueen, further, were designers who had tended to contribute not even to an aesthetic of elegance, but one of grossness, coarseness and ugliness. Comte Hubert de Givenchy said of Galliano and McQueen — his first and second successors at the helm of Maison Givenchy — that their work was a "total disaster. It is neither elegant or new. It means nothing." Their dresses, he said "were unsellable or at least unwearable ... disastrous ... not a representative image of good taste in France ..."[91]

Michael Foale, the second Briton into Space, who had spent several months on the Russian Space-station *Mir*, urged greater British involvement in manned Space-flight, and to support the new international Space station. Mark Hempsell, a specialist in orbital platforms from Bristol University, supported him, stating:

> In the next century space will be the biggest industry the world has. Yet we have nothing to do with launch vehicles, we have nothing to do with the basic space infrastructure.

> Space will be where the energy market is, it will be the place for tourism and travel as well as communications satellites.[92]

However Professor Andre Balogh, a space physics expert at Imperial College London, disagreed, saying: "The UK has to be selective among the extremely sparse resources we have." This was when the country was spending more than £700 million on the Millennium Dome and which the previous year had spent £21 billion on Christmas presents.

On 13 April, 1998, the *Daily Telegraph's* science editor, Roger

Highfield, wrote that a series of British space projects and British participation in international space projects were under threat because of funding cuts, and that one government official had admitted the problems were causing a collapse in university space science research. The British space budget for the year of £196 million was down by £6 million from the previous year, and the recently retired head of the Particle Physics and Astronomy Research Council, Professor Ken Pounds, said Britain was spending 13% less on particle physics and astronomy than it did in 1979/80, with 38% less in the domestic budget. Highfield continued that the Government had already faced revolt from astronomers when it announced closure of the Royal Greenwich Observatory, Britain's oldest science institution, citing cash shortages. The head of the observatory, Dr Jasper Wall, had been threatened with disciplinary action if he spoke out. It appeared to be impossible to find out what Labour's whole science policy was, or indeed if it had one beyond slogans.[93]

In reply to this John Battle, the Minister of State for Science, wrote that Britain was in fact funding more than £25 million worth of new European Space Agency Programmes, and that in the coming years there would be British involvement in ESA projects such as the comet probe Rosetta and the Planck mission. He concluded: "Britain's scientific expertise is respected throughout the world, and we will ensure that we continue to earn that respect."[94]

Certainly, more than £25 million of new funding was the reverse of cuts, but it was tiny compared to, for example, what was being spent on the Millennium Dome. The letter had a junior-partner sound to it, suggesting Britain would have a minor role in projects, which, if it was to preserve any *political* credibility in Europe, it could not very well get out of. There was nothing about new British ventures or British initiatives in Space.

This was the country whose people had played a leading role in practically every major technological invention since the industrial revolution, including television, the computer, radar, and the conception of the communications satellite, which had built the West's first jet fighter and the World's first jet air-liner.

It was, further, nearly 40 years since the first man in space and nearly 25 years since not the first but the last man had landed on the moon. Looked at one way, it was as if it had been beyond Britain's resources to get an aircraft into the air in 1943 — forty years after the Wright brothers' first flight.

The story of the Millennium Dome, described rather gently by A N Wilson as "a monument to humbug and hypocrisy"[95] and by Hugo Young in the Left-wing *Guardian* as "A scandal rising from the swamp of politics" was central to the style, mental atmosphere and cultural strategy of New Labour and the cultural Nomenklatura. Blair himself claimed:

> This is Britain's opportunity to greet the world with a celebration that is so bold, so beautiful, so inspiring, that it embodies at once the spirit of confidence and adventure in Britain and the spirit of future [*sic*] in the world.

> This is the reason for the Millennium Experience: not the product of imagination run wild, but a huge opportunity for Britain. It is good for Britain, so let us seize the moment and put on something of which we and the world will be proud ... We will say to ourselves with pride: this is our Dome, Britain's Dome. And believe me, it will be the envy of the world.

A letter in *The Big Issue*, sold by homeless people on street corners, commented in its Glasgow edition that this last statement was quite correct: the deprived and fund-starved areas of Glasgow would indeed envy such spending.[96]

The bandwagon, Blair said, was already beginning to roll, and on 31 December, 1999, Greenwich would be the most exciting place in the world to be.[97] He claimed further that:

> When I was in the United States people were already talking

about how Britain would be the focus of the world's attention
in the year 2000.[98]

Rome or Bethlehem would not get a look-in. A visit to the Dome,
the Prime Minister claimed, would be "the most exciting day
out in the world."[99]

When these pronouncements were made there was still no
knowledge of what the Dome would contain, or why. At no time
had New Labour or its Conservative predecessor consulted "the
people" on whether they wanted the Dome at all. It was not
difficult to think of all manner of things that the money might
have been spent on, from rescue-archaeology or medical research to some very large one-off project (like the "biosphere"
in the US) which could never be financed by conventional means
or in ordinary times, but which would pay unique dividends in
its own way. A Gallup poll in the *Daily Telegraph* on 14 March,
1998, indicated that only 2% of the population agreed that lottery money should be spent on the Dome. Eighty-four percent
of those interviewed believed the money should be spent on
improving Health or Education. The *Socialist Standard*, organ of
the minuscule Socialist Party, claimed:

> In the world of nightmarish apparitions, there can be few to
> match the vision of the future festering away in the imagination
> of Peter Mandelson MP. He is the high-priest of New Labour's
> dream of a New Britain in which the sordid realities of capital-
> ism evaporate into a mist of slick presentation. Acclaimed ar-
> chitect of the Blairite victory of imagery over experience,
> Mandelson has become a veritable personification of the de-
> scent of ideas (however wrong they were) into ever-evaporating
> froth."[100]

Two governments had made and maintained this huge commitment not only without democratic consultation: it was also
lacking in transparency in the public-accountability sense of the

term — responsibility seemed lost in a Kafkaseque complex of overlapping semi-public and semi-secret government and private bodies and offices.[101] It was another demonstration of *power*, in the Orwellian sense of: "He who controls the past controls the future." The Dome and the other Millennium events would inevitably push a certain political version of British culture and National Identity. This would be not simply a matter of direct content, but of emphasis, omission, context, even such things as lighting and lettering. It cannot be culturally value-neutral.

The Dome and the other Millennium celebrations, along with being a magnificent opportunity for the government to extend patronage to the culturally correct, and to allow them to consolidate their position against any lingering remnants of conservative culture, would potentially be a machine for mummifying traditional National Identity and therefore for killing it. The history that shapes tradition and National Identity is fragile. Mere flippancy can kill it, or its categorisation as "nostalgia." Burke wrote that, without a continuity of knowledge and tradition, no generation could link with the next and humans would live and die as flies of a summer. The effect of relegating everything that had gone before to a museum exhibit, would be to amputate Britain's traditional identity from its present and categorise it as a quaint tourist attraction, like the Natural History Museum of fossils and stuffed animals. This would also fit nicely with Britain's integration into Europe

The *Daily Mail* reported on 22 December, 1997, that the designers of the Millennium Dome had been ordered to make it "more controversial and provocative". A spokesman for the New Millennium Experience Company [*sic*] confirmed that artist Damien Hirst, best known for displaying cut-up animal carcasses as works of art, was working on a project for the Dome,[102] as was the California-based David Hockney, who had previously vowed never to return to Britain. It was then reported the Dome would be "divided like a cake, with each segment representing a 'street' in time". The creative director of the Millennium

Experience, Stephen Bayley, had said in July, 1997, that he did not want "Union Flags" inside the Dome, while Peter Mandelson, the Minister Without Portfolio in charge of the project, said there was no intention "to dwell too much" on the deeds of the British Empire. A 30-foot steel sphere drawn to Earth by a giant magnet would be at the Dome's centre. Mr Bayley was quoted as saying: "It doesn't really mean anything, but gives you a counter-intuitive ... thing." Mr Mandelson himself said:

> The impact of Christianity on Western civilisation will be central to the Millennium experience.[103]

Talking of the impact of Christianity on Western Civilisation was a bit like talking of the impact of Shakespeare on Hamlet. It was astounding that a person in such a position could conceive of speaking in such terms. However, Jennifer Page, the Chief Executive of the Experience, then maintained that the spiritual content had not been finalised, and that it would be necessary to take account of the views of business backers in a multi-faith society. She added that if there is nothing but Christianity in the Dome there would be scope for a lot of people to believe that the "organisation is operating on an exclusive rather than inclusive basis," and further that the content would also be influenced by "particular angles of individual sponsors."[104]

Sir Terence Conran, fashionable restaurateur, Dome consultant and impeccable Blairist, claimed that the Millennium "is not an event which had very much to do with Christianity. It's to do with time."[105] A dominant Christian theme would be "absolutely inappropriate".[106]

There would apparently be a "Spirit Zone", or a "body, mind and spirit zone", one of nine sections of the Dome. However Bayley said it would be a mistake to suggest there would be "an explicit, precise, denominational Christian theme". Bayley resigned shortly after this (or, as A N Wilson unkindly put it, minced off in a huff), accusing Mandelson of acting like a dictator. Bayley

later claimed in his diary for these months, giving a certain illustration of the mental atmosphere of the great project:

> There is some talk of commissioning a mascot for the Millen-
> nium, an idea that seems to me witless and vulgar; therefore
> characteristic, I say at a meeting that if anyone wants a fluffy
> koala in union jack knickers then I am resigning, a prospect I
> view with intense pleasure ... When Mandelson flies off to
> Florida to see Disney (and takes the opportunity of being com-
> prehensively photographed doing so), I decide I have to resign
> for the last time. I don't think Mandy takes me any more seri-
> ously than I take him but introducing Mickey Mouse aesthetics
> into the Dome seems like a calculated insult. My wife says:
> 'Tell them you don't do theme parks.' I do. Typical of the Mil-
> lennium blunder, muddle, chaos and malevolence is that they
> now want to issue a press release about my going ... The Prime
> Minister hosts a Dome presentation ... and orders the nation to
> shut up and enjoy the sordid vulgarity ...[107]

Counter-attacking, Mandelson claimed Bayley had "a tendency
to believe ... only he could get it right ..." He elaborated that:

> If there's one failing we have in our country it is that sometimes
> we are not ambitious enough, we're not confident enough about
> ourselves — great projects, bold and audacious programmes
> or events or constructions are for other countries to do because
> Britain no longer has the capacity or the ambition or the self-
> confidence to pull the thing off. I don't accept that and the
> government doesn't accept that.[108]

Mandelson, evoking "the British way of life", made pilgrimage
to Disneyworld at Florida to obtain further ideas on how to pull
the thing off. There he was presented to Mickey Mouse himself,
and was shown the self-raising lavatory seat of the future. There
were, he said, "only two organisations that can do this sort of
thing and get it right — Disney and Britain". In Disney World
he had seen "so many things to excite your eye and stimulate

your mind".[109] The significant thing was not that the Disney organisation was particularly crass, but that it had come to specialise in manipulating the modern popular mind.

Bayley had supped with an insufficiently long spoon. He complained that he was an elevated, sensitive soul who regarded "typography as far, far more important in the general run of things than politics itself". He believed that if Mandelson received instruction from Mickey Mouse and Donald Duck he should at least have had the grace to do so secretly:

> A covert visit to Florida to experience at first hand Disney's supreme professionalism would have been one thing, but a formal audience with Mickey Mouse for inspirational purposes was, I felt, misjudged ...'[110]

The Millennium Experience, from its budget to its nomenclature, showed, as clearly as anything else, the new regime's blindness to aspects of its own ridiculousness. Further, it seemed to point to a deep-seated inferiority complex: could Britain, with a history and tradition of ritual, pageantry and splendour unequalled by any State, not think of ideas for the Dome for itself? But the great State ceremonies were part of the culture targeted for disappearance and part of the traditional Britain whose amputation from the living present was a large part of Blairism's obsession and *raison d'être*.

Thus, with commitments to spend nearly £800 million on the Dome, the Government apparently still had no clear idea of its format, even the possible role of the Judeo-Christian or Disneyo-Christian heritage. King Ludwig the Mad of Bavaria, when he threw up the castle of Neuschwanstein and other towering follies, at least had a clear purpose and knew what he was doing. Even the increasingly weirdo writer J G Ballard ridiculed it.[111] A *Daily Telegraph* leader commented that:

> It stands for the vacuum of a civilisation that has lost the understanding of what makes it civilised.[112]

In the face of such criticism the Dome Committee responded that the Dome would show a £6 million film called *The Jesus Story*. There would be a puppet of Christ, bound before Pontius Pilate. Later it was announced that the Dome would contain a gigantic statue of a single parent and child, the public being able to walk through the former's body. Mandelson claimed in the *Evening Standard* in December, 1997, that the dome would:

> Make a powerful statement to the rest of the world about Britain's new-found pride and self-confidence. For all these reasons, Tony Blair is driving the project forward. He knows what Britain is capable of achieving.[113]

In June, 1998, the project was clarified a little further. It was announced to the bewildered populace that the figure would be of a bisexual Siamese twin, with male and female torsos but only one head. In July it was announced that the figure would be two-headed but would have only two legs to go with male and female heads and torsos.

Visiting Japan in January, 1998, Blair did not raise the question of compensation for surviving British servicemen who had been Japanese prisoners-of-war, but asked Toyota, Sony, and other Japanese companies for financial investment in the Dome. Japanese firms, it was said, could invest up to £12 million each in sponsorship in return for having their products "showcased" in the Dome, which Mandelson had said would "celebrate our achievements and our talents" and would be a "marvellous opportunity for British manufacturers".

Mandelson claimed he wanted to make the Dome a "spiritual beacon" which would do nothing less than "improve society". It would, he claimed, be "an opportunity for renewal, including spiritual renewal" throughout the country. Christianity, he said, "had shaped our country and our society to a remarkable extent" and admitted that he had once almost become a Christian himself.[114] He apparently failed to notice that London's skyline and river were already well supplied with spiritual beacons, such as Saint Paul's Cathedral. Meanwhile the Church of England announced that it would try to raise £2 million to increase the Christian content of the Dome.[115]

Here we see a central problem of Blairism and New Labour: in so great a dissolution of values and identity that there seems nothing positive left to which they can refer. With traditional positive ideas of beauty out of the question, symbolism is made intentionally ugly. In June, 1998, it was announced that the official symbol of the Millennium Experience would be a pin-headed, thunder-thighed, chicken-beaked effigy of a female, apparently copied from a commercial medicine logo. It was apparently chosen by Mandelson and there had certainly been no nonsense about "the People" being consulted. The *Daily Mail* described it as "like a clumsy piece of primitive cave art,"[116] a quite unfair comment as it was vastly inferior to the evocative Cro-Magnon works preserved in the caves of the Dordogne and Altamira. In its deliberate ugliness it, like the bisexual Siamese twin, was plainly intended as a further frontal attack on traditional ideas of beauty and of traditional culture. It also symbolised shame for past cultural achievements in that half the figure, symbolising the previous millennium, was black. Sir Roy Strong, former director of the Victoria and Albert Museum, commented:

> This logo wipes out all the symbolism of the past, just as the Dome tries to. We have 2,000 years of Britain's past to celebrate and be proud of — 2,000 years of what we've given the world.

Architectural historian Gavin Stamp commented:

> The head doesn't appear to be big enough to hold a brain. in fact this is a brilliant design to sum up modern Britain. It has no purpose, it's empty and vapid, it is obsessed with the body and has no brain.[117]

The "Sensations" art exhibition in late 1997, featured various parodies of the crucifixion and a portrait of Myra Hindley made up of children's finger-prints. The Serpentine Gallery exhibition, opened in February, 1998, in the presence of the Nomenklatura of Cool Britannia, had as a leading exhibit was 32 small tins said to be filled with an artist's excrement. These were further demonstrations of the Nomenklatura's power and of the defeat and impotence of traditional art. The funding of tinned turds was one of many things that took precedence over the survival of the D'Oyly Carte.

The Secretary of State for Culture, Chris Smith, urged the BBC to produce fewer historical dramas by writers like Jane Austen, claiming: "What I would be worried about is that they ended up doing just *Pride and Prejudice*" and claiming further that: "Formulaic historical drama without any real bite isn't going to work for viewers." He wanted more plays with "gritty" social messages about Britain today.[118] On the other hand, Peter Wolff, who came to Britain as a 7-year-old Jewish refugee from Nazism, decided it was necessary to donate £1 million of his own money to set up a trust to support some kind of theatre at the West End not preoccupied with "filth and violence." He said, "I want to see a return to beautiful, traditional plays ..."[119]

Smith claimed: "The distinctions between the higher and popular arts are meaningless." and specified that Bob Dylan was as "valid" as Keats.[120]

* * *

One aspect of the temper of the times was interestingly shown in a leading middle market newspaper which on 14 March, 1998, eloquently denounced sexual promiscuity and teenage pregnancies in a leader headed: "Sowing the seeds of a social crisis." This claimed:

In the bleak statistics of social and personal tragedy, Britain is once again setting new records.

This week's official figures reveal that this country is now at the top of the European league for pregnancy among teenage girls aged between 11 and 15. The tide of teenage abortion is swelling to new heights. Our overall illegitimacy rate is rising at an unprecedented pace.

What a world of human misery lies behind the cold data. Nearly 9,000 girls became pregnant in 1996, when they were little more than children themselves. Whether they opted for an abortion or decided to have their babies, their lives have been blighted.

Yet pitifully little is being done to reverse the trend. The law which supposedly imposes a legal age of consent is rarely enforced. The established church often seems too timid to warn against sin, too ineffectual to talk of moral responsibilities. As for politicians, they long ago ceased to be capable of setting an example ...

It concluded:

Teenagers can engage in sex knowing that not only will there be hardly a word of censure but that their activities are almost approved by liberal opinion. Youngsters have been set adrift without a moral compass. Is it really any wonder if so many of them end up lost and ruined?

The point of quoting this is that the same edition of the same paper that so thundered forth published a two-page feature glamorising and advertising Kylie Minogue, a role-model to many girls and the former mistress of a suicided and drug-addicted rock-star, who had also been the father of an illegitimate child. Miss Minogue was pictured in a series of flattering poses boasting of promiscuity under the heading (far bigger than that of the leader): "I do have one-night stands. Why not? It's cheaper than therapy." The feature concluded by adding helpfully: "The new CD, Kylie Minogue, is due for release on March 23." This was not at all a pro-Blairite paper and was a major critic of Blairism and Cool Britannia, but its behaviour here seemed to

illustrate how media culture and political culture melded to create a pervasive mental atmosphere. Innumerable such examples could be quoted, virtually every day and from across the
whole spectrum of the media. This same paper, so concerned at
the church's lack of concern for moral responsibilities, would a
few days later be reporting details of the trial of an Army officer
accused of sexual misconduct in terms quite indistinguishable
from pornography. This was a wilderness of mirrors. A socially-
conservative rhetoric could be used with some eloquence, but
simultaneously notice was served that the *Zeitgeist* was altogether
elsewhere.

Bruce Anderson commented that:

> Two hundred years ago, many liberals believed that if man-
> kind could only liberate itself from its worship of gods and its
> deference to kings, barbarism would inevitably give way to the
> reign of reason and virtue. In one respect the liberals have had
> their way: gods and kings are not what they were. Instead, we
> have lottery tickets, astrology and pop music.[121]

According to a survey of 8,000 adults in Britain released by the
Centre for the Future of Communications at the University of
Leeds in September, 1997, more than 83% believed science cre-
ated more problems than it solved. More than one in seven believed abduction by aliens was possible. "People are displaying
greater irrationality," the Research Director of the centre said.[122]
If the budget for real Space science fell, newsagents were well-
supplied with UFO and Alien-abduction magazines. Among
the products advertised in these latter was a paste which, if
smeared on the body, would cause Aliens to leave one alone in
disgust (I understand no-one wearing this paste *was* abducted
by Aliens, so it was apparently efficacious). In July, 1998, following England's defeat by Argentina in the World Cup, the Bible
Society, with the backing of the Archbishop of Canterbury, called
on the nation to forgive David Beckenham for being sent off

during the match. Dr David Spriggs, the director of the society
and a Baptist Minister, said: "What is so important is that David
has faced up to his mistake, and asked the forgiveness of his
team-mates and the whole nation ..."[123]

The crisis in British education — with many pupils leaving
school unemployable and huge numbers of teachers quitting in
disgust — had been caused not by too much central supervision
of the curriculum, but by too little. In the past, certainly, teachers in some schools had pushed political agendas in the cur-
ricula with the apparently deliberate intent of unfitting their
pupils (working-class and frequently black) for any kind of work
in Capitalist society and had escaped even noticeable professional discipline, let alone criminal prosecution. Jobs advertised
at University Lecturer level did not carry a living wage for a
family man in a large city.

Niall Ferguson, Fellow of Jesus College, Oxford, wrote:

> Just lately, I have begun to fear that I am living in a neo-medi-
> eval society ... It is the revival of superstition which alarms me
> ... how else are we to explain the huge success of (for example)
> a book such as *The Bible Code*, a ludicrous piece of neo-cabalastic
> claptrap which claims a secret message can be extracted from
> the text of the Scriptures by giving the original letters and words
> numerical equivalents. To my astonishment, this has been one
> of the year's publishing successes.
>
> Until recently, I had always supposed the basic achievements
> of the Enlightenment were pretty secure ... Yet now I realise I
> was too optimistic. For not only are ordinary people reading
> superstitious tosh like *The Bible Code*. Increasingly, they are be-
> having with all the irrationality of medieval peasants ... Of course
> it is always tempting for academics to see irrationalism as a
> perennial feature of popular culture. But the achievements of
> the Enlightenment are under attack in universities, too ...[124]

The Midland Bank decided to dumb-down its arts sponsorship,
giving £1 million to a rock festival, abandoning its long-term
commitment to the Royal Opera House and the Birmingham

Royal Ballet, which a bank spokesman categorised as "elitist and old-fashioned." Another bank, NatWest, sold two panoramas of Eighteenth Century London by Antonio Joli (a contemporary of Canaletto) for £1.7 million to buy so-called "Britart", including works by exhibitors at the Sensations exhibition.[125] The BBC said Frank Muir's best-selling memoirs *A Kentish Lad* were "too literary" to serialise.

Footnotes

88 However, Blake's famous reference to "dark Satanic mills" may have referred not to factories but to universities and the new scientistic learning.

89 *Daily Telegraph*, 5 November 1997

90 *Daily Telegraph*, 4 November 1997

91 *Daily Telegraph*, 15 January 1998

92 *Daily Telegraph*, 19 December 1997

93 See also Highfield's article in the *Daily Telegraph* of 5 November 1997, on the House of Lords Select Committee on Science and Technology's questioning of the Minister on this point.

94 *Daily Telegraph*, 18 April 1998

95 *Daily Telegraph*, 18 January 1998

96 *Big Issue* (Glasgow) March 12-18 1998. It was beside the point that Scotland was in general being heavily subsidised by England.

97 *Daily Telegraph*, 25 February 1998

98 *Sunday Telegraph*, 1 March 1998

99 *Mail on Sunday*, 1 March 1998. Former airline pilot Norman Tebbit commented:"I can guarantee it will be less exciting than an airline flight with Tony Blair's...guests at No 10, the drunken, drug sodden, foul-mouthed Oasis slobs, who have incurred the wrath of Cathay Pacific Airlines.

100 *Socialist Standard,* March 1998 p.4

101 New Labour does not like secret bodies it does not control. It demanded, under threat of Contempt of Parliament, that the Freemasons publish lists of their members involved in the criminal justice system.

102 Mr. Hirst's work received further Government imprimatur when Culture Secretary Chris Smith chose to commission one of his so-called "spin paintings" for the cover of his book *Creative Britain*.

103 *Daily Telegraph,* 6 January 1998

104 *Daily Telegraph,* 6 January 1998

105 *Times,* 13 January 1998

106 *Daily Telegraph,* 26 January 1998

107 *Guardian,* 13 April 1998

108 *Daily Telegraph,* 14 January 1998

109 *Daily Mail,* 5 January 1998

110 *Spectator,* 17 January 1998

111 *Daily Telegraph,* 17 January 1998

112 *Daily Telegraph,* 24 December 1997

113 Quoted by Matthew d'Ancona, *Sunday Telegraph,* 4 January 1998

114 *Daily Telegraph,* 14 January 1998

115 *Daily Telegraph,* 24 February 1998

116 *Daily Mail,* 5 June 1998

117 *Daily Mail,* 5 June 1998

118 *Daily Telegraph,* 2 March 1998

119 *Daily Mail,* 2 February 1998

120 *Spectator,* 28 March 1998

121 *Spectator,* 13 September 1998

122 *Daily Telegraph,* 5 September 1997

123 *Daily Telegraph,* 10 July 1998

124 *Daily Telegraph,* 11 November 1997

125 *Daily Telegraph,* 26 February 1998

Chapter 5 The Ghouls' Carnival

A few hours before I was due to leave Australia for a long dreamed-of extended visit to Britain, I heard of the death of Diana, Princess of Wales, with the normal sadness one feels for any young life cut short, and with sympathy for her family.

In Singapore I saw the first of the madness. The *Straits Times* reported with some bemusement that the British press were demanding the Royal Family "Show Grief" and that the Queen and Prince of Wales should "break down, cry and hug one another on the steps of Westminster Abbey."

This, I thought, is crazy. If true, it is evil. But it is too crazy, it implies too gross a violation of ordinary human conduct and values, to be true. I thought of how, when I had lost members of my own family, I had valued two things above all: the support of close friends and privacy to mourn in my own way. If it was true, there was something fascist here, something like the confessions and break-down of a Stalinist show-trial, the demand that all privacy and integrity be ripped away to appease "The People". Morally this behaviour by the media seemed not unlike a killer railing at the lack of grief shown by the victim's family.

I came back to where I was. The surroundings were eminently sane. I was reading the paper in a modern, well-appointed hotel. Outside was a busy construction site. The neat, white-shirted men and smartly-dressed women passing outside were part of a world which was not mine, but which, within its own

terms, made eminent sense. I visited the Battle Box, the recently
re-opened British army underground headquarters from World
War II, and laughed with my taxi-driver over shared memories
of *The Gods Must be Crazy*. The *Straits Times* must have misunder-
stood. Still, I kept the cutting when I boarded my plane.

I didn't know the half of it.

I arrived in Britain a few hours before The Funeral. In a
sense, it was the ambition of any provincial writer: to be present
at a History-making event. It would be a weirdly appropriate
introduction to a bizarre new Britain under a bizarre new social
and cultural order. It was a carnival of ghoulish madness reminiscent of what I have read of the Medieval plagues and the
Chiliastic panics at the end of the First Millennium.

"Show Us You Care!" screamed the front-page headline of
the *Express*, alongside a file-picture of the Queen looking cold
and remote (six months later there would not be an atom of
rebuke for the Queen continuing her official duties the day Princess Margaret had a stroke). The *Sun*, a major contributor to
the paparazzi-culture and celebrity sleaze-mongering which had
probably caused the fatal car-wreck, demanded: "Where is the
Queen when the country needs her?" and claimed that it was
"The final insult" that there should not be any flag over Buckingham Palace (the Queen happened to be away at the time).
Later Stephen Glover wrote:

> The most odious moral assumption of the past few days has
> been the assumption that the grief of members of the public is
> comparable to — and sometimes greater than — the grief of
> the Princess's immediate family. The sight of people queuing
> to sign books of condolence has been deeply affecting, but it is
> surely a form of madness to equate their sorrow with that of
> her bereaved relatives ...

The *Sunday Mirror* claimed in a tirade against the Royal Family
that: "The people of Britain are suffering grievously". Like the

other British tabloids it had been — and would continue to be
— an international leader of and market for the intrusive, vio-
lating, paparazzi-culture. The media claimed a victory in forcing the Queen to emerge, to go on public mournabout to show
herself and to display her bereaved grandsons to the ghoulish
gaze of The People. This was headlined, not in the tabloids but
in the *Times*, as "Diana's army cheers victory". It continued
that the Royal Family "bows to public pressure to show its
grief".[126] The *Sunday Times* claimed in a huge double-page spread
that "Palace Bows to the People's Will". It went on in the same
weird proto-Totalitarian language that:

> Britain's collective grief turned to anger last week as the royal
> family clung to their Scottishfastness ... The Queen was un-
> knowing and unyielding. She has been severely jolted by the
> public reaction ...[127]

The *Telegraph's* version was "Queen bows to her people"[128]. I do
not think that anyone, no matter how much history, politics, or
for that matter science-fiction, they had read, could have imagined so vast and apparently unanimous a departure from ordinary civilised notions of sanity and decency. The whole thing
truly did stink weirdly of a Soviet show-trial, not least because
the Accuseds' presumed guilt had, quite patently, no connection with any events in the real world. But Soviet show-trials
had logic and purpose. This seemed infused with a madness of
a different order.

It was not only the sleaze-peddlers. There appeared to be an
agreement among a number of normally intelligent commentators to take leave of taste and judgement. Mother Teresa had
died in the meantime, and was depicted in a newspaper cartoon
as a sort of humble acolyte helping (or being helped by) Diana
into Heaven. I almost expected someone to claim she had died
of grief for her, and then someone did. Geoffrey Wheatcroft
wrote later: "I skittishly told a friend that there would be visions

of Diana before the week was out — and so there were."[129]

The *Spectator*, which prides itself on cool-headed cynicism, apologised for having run an advertisement for Mercedes cars. The *Evening Standard* claimed that "The people of Paris are weighed down by guilt."[130]

Historian Ben Pimlott, Professor of Politics at London University and member of the Fabian Society executive, announced: "You cannot be a sentient human being and not feel grief and horror." William Rees-Mogg, former editor of *The Times* and one of Britain's foremost public intellectuals, claimed that he left the funeral service stunned and hardly able to think coherently.

Paul Johnson claimed: "It is not often an entire people speak. And they are asking that a woman, cast out in life, be listened to in death. A new spirit is moving across this country." He continued:

> In all sincerity, and at the risk of seeming blasphemous, I am reminded of the Blessed Virgin who, told of her destiny, answered with proud modesty, "I am the handmaiden of the Lord ..." All the original saints of the ecclesiastical calendar were chosen not by Popes and officials in Rome, but by popular acclamation.

Perhaps the original saints had lived somewhat different lives. He continued:

> The surge of feeling ... has been a spontaneous collective religious act by the Nation. It is a plea: "Give us a spiritual dimension, make our lives meaningful. Show us there is more to existence than getting and spending, earning and acquiring. For Diana's sake — for she got the point — tell us that life has a purpose and give us an idea what that purpose is ..."[131]

Apparently under the impression that the Prince of Wales had been driving the fatal car he claimed:

> Prince Charles may be a penitent and changed man — let us
> hope he is — but he remains a tarnished figure and some guilt
> will always cling to him.

Months later Johnson claimed: "I now pray to her" as to Dr
Johnson and Jane Austen,[132] yet Johnson seemed in normal circumstances a profoundly sane, wise and intelligent man.

Piers Paul Reid argued that the death would bring a renewed
respect for the Christian tradition (as distinct, presumably, from
a renewed respect for the use of seat-belts. Just how those well-
known Christians Mohamed and Dodi al-Fayed fitted in otherwise was unclear) "and rebirth of our sense of awe at the
incomprehensible mysteries of the human condition".

He continued: "The comparison has already been made with
Eva Peron; but an equally convincing comparison could be made
with the Virgin Mary."[133]

Left-wing television writer John Mortimer QC, iconoclasm
thoroughly abandoned, compared the funeral to that of the Duke
of Wellington (the actual connection being that the body passed
briefly under the arch of a house the Duke had once lived in).

Clive James recalled the Princess's adulterous and techni-
cally treasonous lover, James Hewitt: "think of where he is now,
deprived of even the reason for his ruin, his empty head already
rotting on Traitors' Gate"[134] which seemed a rather tactless re-
minder that it takes two to tango.

In the *Sunday Telegraph* (The *Telegraph* group were by and large
the sanest papers) she was: "A magnetic life-force".[135]

On 8 September the *Times* headlined "Monarchy will change
— Blair."

Papers (as they had already begun doing in Australia when I
left) raved at "loathsome" paparazzi they had paid. Denounc-
ing media intrusion, the *Daily Mail* published a covertly-obtained
photograph of the Prince of Wales with the caption "Charles
weeps bitter tears of guilt". The tabloids were in general simply

beneath readability even in the line of research. *The News of the World's* "Now you belong to Heaven" was enough.

Ian Corfield of the Fabian Society claimed that Diana was loved because she represented a "genuine feeling of meritocracy." To quote Geoffrey Wheatcroft again:

> She did *what?* The daughter of a rich dipsomaniac earl, whose highest academic achievement was a school prize for best-kept hamster, who married a prince and who died during (and in a sense because of) a liaison with a coke-snorting, starlet-bonking playboy?[136]

Possibly the death and funeral of Nelson had led to a comparable manifestation of public grief. The madness reached the judicial system: two elderly ladies from Czechoslovakia, caught taking teddy-bears from the piled-up tributes, were sentenced to a month's prison, the prosecutor claiming the offence was not far from grave-robbing. For people from a formerly Stalinist State the experience must have been particularly terrifying. The sentence, the magistrate said, must reflect public outrage, harkening back to a jurisprudence previously associated with Pontius Pilate.[137] The sentence was reduced on appeal by a judge after they had spent two nights behind bars. The judge accepted that they had intended only to preserve the teddy-bears as a tribute to Diana and that their action had been innocent, but still fined them £200.00 each, speaking of Britain's "compassion". My own experience of Court of Petty Sessions work in Australia was that first offenders of previous good character convicted of such minor offences could expect a good chance of getting off with a caution or at worst of being fined the equivalent of about one-fifth of this sum. A Sardinian who took a teddy-bear was merely fined £100.00 and then beaten up outside the court.[138] Mr Mark Woodsworth, aged 31, and about to marry, was so overcome that he hanged himself. His father said: "Everything seemed all right until he watched the funeral."

A man from Leeds revealed on a radio phone-in: "My wife died in April ... and I've shed more tears for Diana than I did for my wife." Another man said he felt more grief for Diana than he had for his father's death. It was, as Geoffrey Wheatcroft said, emotional derangement.

In the *Daily Telegraph* Christine Doyle bravely reassured readers that the mourning need not "have a damaging impact on the collective psyche and our physical health." However, there was a "marked rise" in calls to the helplines of the Samaritans and Mind, the mental health charity. According to Mind, "Some callers wanted a national Diana Helpline. We felt this would have been a good idea." It was reported that children were asking, "Mummy, are you going to die?"[139] Religious writer Clifford Longley asked: "Was Cardinal Hume praying to Diana as Catholics pray to Saints?" He continued: "There is no threat to Christianity in a Cult of Diana ... given that the basis of the cult would be her own dedication to the welfare of the least fortunate, only good could come of it." Some of the turn-arounds suggested the change of Communist Party Line when the Nazi-Soviet pact was signed. A columnist who gushed about Diana's qualities as a mother had, hours before, been castigating her for the example she was setting her sons by being photographed while being groped, half-naked, by a paunchy playboy.

On the morning of the funeral London was deserted. I walked through utterly empty streets. I have seen London in mid-winter, in the Christmas-New Year break when the shops are closed and the tourists leave, but it was not as empty as this.

The media anger and hatred directed against the Queen and the Prince of Wales probably had little to do with sublimated guilt over the fact the mass-media culture had caused the death. The hunting-down of such people, particularly lonely and vulnerable intellectuals like Prince Charles, is actively pleasant. Prince Charles occupied a scapegoat's role not unlike that successively occupied by Simon, Piggy and Ralph in *Lord of the Flies*. Oleg Gordievsky wrote:

Throughout the whole of last week I experienced a feeling of *déjà vu*. Finally another week of mourning came back to me: namely the week which took place in the Soviet Union in March 1953 after the death of Joseph Stalin, when a massive and unrestricted brainwashing campaign by the media and the government wrought the populace into a state of hysteria and idolisation.

A bare recital of facts shows the insanity into which a national culture had been plunged. It was later estimate that by 9 September *10,000 tons* of flowers had been piled outside Buckingham Palace and Kensington Palace. This did not count huge deposits at war memorials and other commandeered shrines throughout the country. An application was made to the International Star Registry to have a star named after Diana, another to have a star in the Lyrae Constellation named "Dodi and Diana — Eternally loved." The Chancellor of the Exchequer, Gordon Brown, was said to be seriously considering renaming the August Bank Holiday Diana Day. The press clipping agency Durrants said the coverage of the event by the world's magazines and newspapers far exceeded *any other event in history*.[140]

Indeed it was true, as I had read half-disbelievingly a world away, that the thoroughly progressive *Independent* said it would welcome the sight of the Royal Family in tears and holding on to one another on the steps of Westminster Abbey. This was probably correct — there was no compunction about the bereaved sons, who were to be put through the hoops in public for the sake of The People and circulation.

Private Eye published a cover suggesting elements of public hypocrisy. It was widely banned at newsagencies, apparently because individual newsagency managers feared reprisals from The People. Other dissenters from the ghoulish carnival were, quite literally, intimidated against speaking out.

Previous sacrilege recoiled upon its authors. Steven Glover

in the *Telegraph* pointed out that in September, 1996, the *Daily Mail* had referred to the late Princess's bottom, and had compounded this offence by stating that it was too large for her jeans. In previous issues, he continued, it had discussed her cleavage. In April it had raised the question of her cellulite. The US *National Enquirer* wrote in words whose back-handed honesty deserve to be immortalised:

> We apologise for the Princess Diana Page One headline "Di goes sex mad", which is still on the stands at some locations. It is currently being replaced with a special 72-page tribute issue: "A farewell to the Princess we all loved: Diana — Her Final Hours."

Quoting this later, the *Daily Mail* sternly categorised the *National Enquirer* as "a trashy American tabloid".

William Hague suggested Heathrow Airport be renamed after her, and was criticised for the moderation of the proposal. He was further execrated for saying Blair was mulcting the tragedy for political gain (Parliament's contribution at the Funeral might in other times have been made by the Speaker of the House of Commons, but was made by Blair himself, with broken voice and trembling lip).

The *Observer*, as well as re-publishing a particularly vile piece on the Royal Family, claimed: "Tony Blair spoke for England, for the new England not afraid to show what we feel."[141] The press grovelled too — at least very temporarily — before the Earl Spencer and his attack on the tabloids and on the Royal Family at the funeral service, some implying this was a healthy Feudal revolt of the good English aristocracy against the usurping German Windsors — *nothing* seemed too mad or divorced from ordinary dignity or decency to print. The *Sunday Times* claimed that the applause following the Earl's speech signified a New World Order. Historian and novelist George MacDonald Fraser said later:

What C S Forester so cruelly and accurately described
as lower-deck sentimentality had a field day. Mr Blair
felt proud. I felt ashamed.

Perhaps it was the contrast between the vast carpets of
flowers outside the palaces, and the modest, decent tributes laid at the cenotaphs each November; perhaps it
was the reflection that a heroic figure second to none in
our century, Churchill, received no such monumental
outpourings of grief at his passing — and wouldn't have
wanted it ...[142]

For progressive commentator David Edgar the week of
madness was: "open, soft, organic and — as the candles
lit up London in the small hours of Saturday — turned
night into day. It was also, essentially, collective ... The
people who made what Martin Jacques has dubbed 'The
floral revolution' were engaged in a political act." This
was true, even if incomplete. Public life had entered an
area where the political and the mystical came clammily
and ominously together in the exaltation of unreason.

Arthurian mythology was evoked. When Diana's body
was buried on a lake island, she became "The Lady of
the Lake". (Australian Academic Patrick Morgan has
analysed this in a brilliant article in *The Adelaide Review*.
No British journal seems to have had the perception —
or perhaps courage — to take it up). The *Observer* wrote:

Some idea of the intensity of worship to be expected
emerged yesterday ... A swarm of wasps entered the
floral tributes banked outside the gates of Althorp House
to savour whatever nectar remained. Two children
screamed 'The bees are eating the Princess!' Their
mother, panic-stricken at the sacrilege, rushed to the
bouquets and wreaths ...

Yes, I had been present at an epoch-making event — how else can you describe an event which consumed more media-space internationally than any other in history?

Footnotes

126 *Times,* 5 September 1997
127 *Sunday Times,* 7 September 1997
128 *Daily Telegraph,* 5 September 1997
129 Geoffrey Wheatcroft, "Annus Memorabilis", *Prospect,* January 1998, pp 25-28
130 *Evening Standard,* 5 September 1997
131 *Daily Mail,* 6 September 1997
132 *Spectator,* 3 January 1998
133 *Evening Standard,* 6 September 1997
134 *Sunday Telegraph,* 14 September 1997
135 *Sunday Telegraph,* 7 September 1997
136 *op.cit.* p.28. One feature made the probably unintentionally deadly comment that "clothes were her vocabulary, and over the years she learnt to speak her mind to extraordinary effect" (*Telegraph Magazine,* 14 March 1998)
137 *Daily Telegraph,* 12 September 1997
138 *Daily Telegraph,* 12 September 1997
139 *Sunday Telegraph,* 21 September 1997
140 "Night and Day" *Mail on Sunday Review,* 28 December 1997
141 *Observer,* 7 September 1997
142 *Daily Telegraph,* 3 January 1998

Chapter 6 The Blood-Dimmed Tide

Edward Heathcote-Amory in the *Spectator* summed part of the Dianamania up correctly: the media hoped to drown public wrath in a sea of tributes, while creating an alternative scapegoat — stuffy royals at the head of an antiquated establishment — for an angry populace to blame.[143] However, it was more than this: the media, representing a major part of the cultural Nomenklature, were beaming out the message that in their way they were of the masters now: they were displaying that they could manipulate not just the masses but a goodly part of the intellectual élite into whatever posture they chose.

Since New Labour existed in a close symbiotic relationship with much of the media there was no reason for the Government to find this disagreeable in the short term. However there was an unspoken sub-text for the government to take note of. The media was also saying: "We can do this to the Queen and the Prince of Wales. We can do this too you." For the moment, however, the broad cultural alliance held. Both for the Left and for the Murdoch press, as well as for various individual journalists, it was a chance to push Republicanism. It was also a chance for the Government to further weaken the monarchy and further reduce it to a dependency.

It was also a chance to capitalise on the Conservatives' at least temporary political impotence by demonstrating conservatism's cultural impotence. Respect for the Monarchy had, in modern times, been near the heart of British conservative political values. C S Lewis was not being controversial or taking an unusual position when he wrote on the Coronation in 1953 in terms suggesting the event retained contact with the numinous:

> You know, over here people did not get that fairy-tale feeling about the coronation. What impressed most who saw it was the fact that the Queen herself appeared to be quite over-whelmed by the sacramental side of it. Hence, in the specta-tors, a feeling of (one hardly knows how to describe it) — awe — pity — pathos — mystery. The pressing of that huge, heavy crown on that small, young head becomes a sort of symbol of the situation of *humanity* itself: humanity called by God to be his vice-regent and high priest on earth, yet feeling so inad-equate. As if He said "In my inexorable love I shall lay upon the dust that you are glories and dangers and responsibilities beyond your understanding" ... One has missed the whole point unless one feels that we have all somehow been crowned and that coronation is somehow, if splendid, a tragic splendour ...[144]

At least until the late 1970s the following aspects of the relation-ship between the Monarchy and the people had probably been broadly taken for granted:

1.   The Queen was highly respected, and indeed to the extent that she was seen as the Symbol of the Nation and the Font of Honour, some term higher than "respect" may be ap-propriate;

2.   It was acknowledged that one of the duties of the Royal Family and those who joined it (the Queen Mother, for ex-ample, who had been a commoner before her marriage) was to "set a good example". The Queen (and the Queen mother) had done this faultlessly;

3.   Coronation was a Sacrament, the Queen was head of the established Church, and the Queen and to a lesser extent the other members of the Royal Family were religious as well as secular personages;

4.   The Royal Family were mostly hard-working, and despite the pomp and privilege attached to it, the strains and duties

of Royal life meant that life was not particularly enviable. Older generations at least at some level remembered the premature death of King George VI after the strains of the war years;

5. Media intrusiveness on the Royal Family *as private human beings* was limited, and anything else would have been regarded as intolerable. They were already constantly exposed as public personages;

6. The convention that the Royal Family did not sue for libel was not much abused and was balanced by the fact that libellous material about the Royal Family was seldom if ever published;

7. Not only was the Queen widely accepted as Symbol of the Nation, but also seen as a symbol of national unity. It was no coincidence that as attacks on the Royal Family began to be orchestrated in the 1980s they were sometimes accused of being German, despite the fact all members of the Royal Family able to do so had served in British uniform in the World Wars. George VI had been a midshipman at Jutland with battle-cruisers blown to bits all about him. His brother, the Duke of Kent, had died on active service in World War II. For these and other reasons the Monarchy was not and could not possibly be, involved in Party politics;

8. The military aspects of the institution of Monarchy had not entirely disappeared. Members of the Royal Family frequently appeared in military uniforms and held service ranks. It was taken for granted that their duties included such matters as launching ships and inspecting troops, and that they should possess real as well as ceremonial military skills and should if physically able undertake real military training. Representatives of the monarch, such as Lord Lieutenants and colonial and Commonwealth Governors were frequently senior military officers. In wartime, even in modern times, they had a definite military role;

9. Monarchy and the Royal Family were interwoven with the nation's history in a special way. This was not affected at all by the fact that much of the pageantry associated with

Royalty was relatively new. The House of Windsor had taken its name recently, but its lineage was connected to the dawn of English history;

10. Monarchy was a focus of the positive;

11. Such institutions of Monarchy as the Royal Yacht were examples and displays of the best Britain could do.

These and other factors gave the institution of monarchy an affinity with cultural conservatism. Now cultural conservatives were shown that the Monarch and the Royal Family could be insulted and subjected to all manner of indignity and emotional torture with impunity. It was a complex and multi-directional cultural offensive.

But it was not complete. Media attempts to turn outrage from itself to the Royal Family were not all-conquering. By 13 September, 40,000 people crowded into Hyde Park for the last night of the proms to sing God Save the Queen.

By then barrow-boys were already marketing Diana T-shirts like Guns 'n' Roses concert mementoes with the slogan, packing two falsehoods and one blasphemy into six words: "Born a princess, died a Saint" (nor was the subsidiary saint wholly forgotten: a load of previously unsaleable ET dolls was wrapped in blue and white saris and offered as effigies of Mother Teresa).

A few days later, Cheltenham Borough Council suggested demolishing its dilapidated bus shelter to create a Diana memorial garden. A former Mayor, Ms Pat Thornton, threatened to ride naked through the streets in protest. In the face of this prospect, the idea was dropped. Soon journalist Peter Bradshaw, would be complaining about the brutes and the "patrician conservative press" who were embarrassing him by quoting back what he had written about Diana "In that terrible week":

Yes, It is embarrassing. I suffered from this terribly at a party at the end of last year, when my friend Mark Steel, the stand-up comic and columnist, delighted in quoting to me from memory a particularly delirious piece I had penned for *The Modern Review* having just watched the funeral on television. Reading my tremulous words made him quite incapable with laughter, I am sorry to say, and he laughed a good deal reciting them again, while my face went as purple as my prose. Others recounted similar experiences.[145]

The media's brief self-flagellation over "intrusiveness" was never anything but a ritualised pantomime. The market for paparazzi-pictures fell at least temporarily but nothing about the media's essential culture of intrusiveness and titillation changed.

The *Independent on Sunday* of 19 October, 1997, attempted a huge beat-up headlined: "Was Diana Murdered?" It was, of course, able to produce no evidence at all in support of this proposition, apart from the fact that Diana "once reportedly confided in friends" that "One day I'm going to go up in a helicopter and it'll just blow up. MI5 will do away with me." As the festive season approached, one magazine cover-story was that it would be The First Christmas Without Diana. Other magazines devoted exclusively to Dianamainia appeared on newsagents' racks along with the UFOlogy, astrology and the mammary equipment of Melinda Messenger. It was not intellectual snobbery of the kind rightly condemned by Professor Carey to find all this alarming. It did look like an outbreak of something from the Dark Ages, when, as Chesterton put it, the civic institutions of Rome had evaporated and the soldier of civilisation was no longer fighting Goths but goblins. On 29 December, 1997, Television Channel Four broadcast a programme described in the guide as:

Looking Like Diana: Three Princess Diana lookalikes consider their career options after the death of their role model and reveal their response to the tragedy.

Reveal their responses, forsooth!

On 5 January, 1998, the BBC described the island where the

corpse was buried as "Diana's final home." If I began speaking
of the Fremantle Cemetery as, say, "My great-uncle's final home"
I would expect my friends and family to begin taking one another aside for a serious talk about me.

There was another aspect of this that nobody seemed to notice: the demonstration effect. The message the media was beaming out was that from now on fame, regard, esteem, had nothing
to do with merit, rather the reverse — it had to do with a sort of
glamour that was really only another word for manipulative
neurosis. Every magazine cover-story devoted to Dianamania
excluded from celebration some other person who might be
genuinely meritorious and an exemplar in the old sense. Even
normal members of the Royal Family, not perfected saints but
hard-working and conscientious like the Princess Royal, were
pushed from the stage.[146]

One of the many inexplicable things about this was that no-
one in my own circle of friends, which is fairly wide, or in my
children's circles, which are even wider and twenty years younger
— in fact no-one I met at all — seemed to *actually join in* the
extravagant grief. Indeed in my children's circles the madness
was being sent up and ridiculed from almost Day One. Diana
jokes were flourishing on the Internet — the very essence of that
modernity which Blairism so craved.

In January, 1998, it was announced that The Grave would
be opened by the Spencer family for public inspection, at a cost
of £9.50 a head. For a family of four, this would be £29, more
than a visit to Buckingham Palace, the great museums or the
Tower of London, making it one of the most expensive tourist
attractions in Britain. The day after the announcement, tel-
ephone calls were jammed by eight million calls from people
seeking to buy tickets.[147] Last time I was in Jerusalem, admission
to the Holy Sepulchre was free.

Six months after the tragedy, the *Daily Mail* would be writing
in terms intended to suggest the late Princess had been a literal
miracle worker even while on Earth, having apparently cured a

female fashion journalist (who else?) of cancer by radiating a "white light". *The Mail on Sunday* claimed in large type:

> Liz Tilbris is one of the most remarkable British women of her age ... She became the most powerful woman writer in fashion — only to discover she was on the brink of death ... Now, in a searingly-candid autobiography, she tells how she gained inner strength from Diana's healing powers ...[148]

The whole episode was, among other things, a strange experience of Mob rule as modified for the Twenty-First Century. The mob, it was true, was being manipulated by cleverer people working out their own agenda, but that had probably been true of almost every mob in history. It was a strange mob, demanding — well, demanding something, though nobody seemed to know what, a generally affluent mob, better off materially than the British have ever been before, yet in some way emotionally maimed, empty and desperate, without values or judgement and without mental or emotional strength or dignity. A soft mob, squishy: herbivores like ill-kept hamsters turned vicious from overcrowding and boredom, yammering at the loss of the Great Hamster-Keeper. "Floral Fascism" somebody called it later.

Basically, it seemed, a mob composed of individuals without inner resources demanding an orgy of grief for a person they had never known. Were these strange, wailing creatures really the grand-children of the people who had stoically accepted the probability of total national destruction in war rather than surrender to Hitler?

A day or so later we visited the Natural History Museum, built in the high tide of Nineteenth-Century scientific romanticism as a secular cathedral to challenge the ancient Christian cathedrals of the land. The great marble statues of Darwin and Huxley gazed down at the screaming proletarianised nose- and navel-pierced tattooed anthropoids sprawled on the steps and the divorced fathers dragging their children through the dinosaur galleries because there was nowhere else to take them on access days.

The Dianamania soon merged with the equally fraudulent emotional manipulation of the film *Titanic*. Indeed, as that film drew to a close amid the sobs of the juvenile female audience one expected to see the deceased Princess bobbing radiantly among the plastic frozen corpses. The confluence of these two *ersatz* grief-wallowings was neatly symbolised when a replica of a jewel worn by Kate Winslet in the film was sold for US \$2.2 million (£1,325,000) at a Beverley Hills fund-raiser in aid of the Princess Diana Memorial Fund.

Carpets of flowers had been laid down, but when I arose before the sweepers one Sunday morning shortly after, the streets a few yards away were almost as thickly and literally carpeted with litter, vomit and broken bottles.

Bruce Anderson wrote that "Many people feel that they no longer understand their own countrymen."[149]

However, despite the continuing media obsession, there were signs of the Dianamania dying away. In April, 1998, it was reported that people were refusing Diana stamps at post offices.[150] By June or July there was a feeling abroad that many more people were becoming heartily sick of it — although this was revealed mainly in private conversations and after a precautionary glance over the shoulder.

At the funeral the two young princes, bereft of their mother in appallingly public circumstances, disappointed the *Independent* by not breaking down in tears and hugging one another on the steps of the Abbey. They walked dignified and dry-eyed in the funeral procession. This hearkened back to an older world in which there was a certain fundamental seriousness of being and therefore of behaviour.

Yet it could not be dismissed as a transient episode of madness, group mania or Chiliastic panic. What the whole thing demonstrated was not republican or anti-monarchical sentiment either, but a vast confusion of traditions and values. It was a demonstration of, among other things, how far traditional norms of behaviour had been eroded. The *Spectator* would write later:

> The public outcry against Deiride Rachid's sentence for fraud in Coronation Street told us more about contemporary British mores than the social surveys of the past decade. For the benefit of innocents, a middle-aged woman character in Coronation Street — the mother of all "soaps" — is given a prison sentence for fraud; the public is outraged and a Labour MP from the North-East has raised the matter with the Home Secretary. Add to this the weight given to football and its millionaire players and the adulation of women boxers, and we see the outlines of our post-Christian society.[151]

Footnotes

143 *Spectator*, 20 September 1997

144 C.S. Lewis, *Letters to an American Lady*, William B.Eerdmans, Michigan, 1971, pp 18-19

145 *Evening Standard*, 13 January 1998

146 It is interesting to note a comment by Lynda Lee-Potter in the *Daily Mail* of January 21 1998: "The very idea that children would want to be cuddled by a complete stranger I find utterly amazing, especially in front of the press, says Princess Anne. Last year she carried out 642 engagements without cuddles, hugs and kisses. She was brisk, efficient and utterly professional. She gives no picture opportunities. She's never talked about her anguish, inner pain or personal therapies. In 30 years time she will no doubt look very much as she does today, which is weather-beaten, grim faced, built to last and proof that the Royals survive best when they inspire respect not worship."

147 *Daily Mail*, 8 January 1998

148 *Mail on Sunday*, 8 March 1998

149 *Spectator*, 13 September 1997

150 *Daily Telegraph,* 21 April 1998
151 *Spectator,* 4 April 1998

Chapter 7 Star Wars and Aliens:
a Case-Study

Fashions in fiction, story-telling and entertainment are closely relevant to all this. Those words: "we see the outlines of our post-Christian society" seem to hang in the air.

The contrasting *Star Wars* and *Aliens* films (American-made to be sure, but important in British culture now) are worth examining here. The original *Star Wars* and *Alien* film trilogies, and the now quite extensive book-publishing spin-offs from them, each add up to a fairly complete but quite contrasting view of the human condition. They also offer useful broad summaries of two of the major positions in cultural conflict: the conservative and the sensation-driven Nihilist.

The first episode of both trilogies was released in the late 1970s, both achieved the status of science-fiction classics, and both have been seen by everyone with the remotest interest in the genre as well as by millions who don't normally touch science-fiction. Each is, by accident or design, a genuine trilogy, with organic development not unlike that of the old three-volume novel. Both support spin-off industries, and in each case new episodes have been or are about to be released.

However the differences between them are striking. It a sense they sum up much of the cultural conflict taking place not only in Britain (with the government as a to some extent ambiguous participant) but in all that part of the world now coming under the influence of international mass culture. They might even be described as summing up much of the mythologies of traditional Western — and indeed Judeo-Christian — culture, and the so-far discernible shape of post-Christian culture.

Star Wars is basically conservative in values: family love is a redeeming force, virtue is rewarded and the past has wisdom for the present. The good and bad sides of the "force" are not, in *Star Wars*, equal as they would be in a Dualistic Universe, even though the protagonists appear during the course of the story to believe they are. The dark side is, the sage Yoda warns, "quicker, easier, more seductive" than the good side, but the good side still triumphs against all odds and even contrary to the expectations of the best and wisest of the good people.

Moreover, it transpires that Evil does not have an independent existence: the wicked Darth Vader is a good man gone wrong, still at his worst justifying his position by appealing to values, such "ending this destructive conflict", and bringing "order" to the Galaxy, which are anything but evil in themselves.

It is also an exuberant Universe. The weird creatures in it, while impossible to take completely seriously, seem a tribute to richness and diversity, suggesting the Galaxy is full of surprises and a wonderful place for adventures. I think Chesterton would have liked the spoof aliens in the dive at Mos Eisley (even apart from the fact the unkind might suggest that he physically resembled some of them). The evil creatures often have a comic element about them (is it drawing too long a bow to suggest that George Lucas may, like Dante in his description of Satan, feel Evil has a ridiculous aspect?). Similarly, Poul Anderson wrote recently that he had written the Dominic Flandry series of SF novels in part "to convey some feeling of how endlessly varied and wonderful the universe is in which we live".

There is very little sex in the *Star Wars* films, apart from some shots of Princess Leia scantily attired as Jabba the Hutt's prisoner. In considerable contrast to the sexual sadism and necrophilia of the Alien industry (of which more below), this particular episode is strikingly normal.

Princess Leia behaves bravely and resourcefully, and, as a princess should, keeps her dignity under stress. *Proper* hierarchy and degree are respected. The view of social organisation appears to be the classically Western one of "Take but degree away, untune that string, and hark what discord follows." Socially and politically conservative publications such as *The Illustrated London News* and *The American Spectator* were generally benign in their reviews of *Star Wars* even when they did not specifically analyse it politically. Left-wing publications and such as the *New Statesman* and the US *Nation*, attacked it, sometimes in extraordinarily extravagant terms.

The politics of *Star Wars* are by implication anti-totalitarian. That they are basically in accord with a Burkean conservatism, as I have argued in *Return of the Heroes; "The Lord of the Rings", "Star Wars" and Contemporary Culture*, Hal Colebatch, (Australian Instituteof Public Policy, Perth, Western Australia, 1990). The rebels against the evil Empire (as in *The Lord of the Rings* which in many ways it resembles) are a heterogeneous group. They include a princess, a wise knight, a free-booting smuggler, a crook-turned-businessman and various aliens and robots. A Communist publication in the last days of the Cold War attacking *Star Wars* as being advocacy for political pluralism and "free enterprise special pleading" was quite insightful.

Otherwise disparate, the good side are able to unite in opposition to the totalitarian ideal of "progress" as meaning progress towards power rather than progress towards liberty. Behind them seem to be beliefs and values like those of Burke that all that is necessary for the triumph of evil is that good men do nothing, and that the traditions and values of the past give strength and purpose to the present. If men are not to be as flies of a summer, one generation must link with another. Thus, Luke Skywalker wants to be true to his good father's memory, and it is a solemn and portentous moment when he inherits his father's old lightsaber. The Princess is defended by Luke with a chivalry that might be inspired by Burke's famous passage on the fate of Marie Antoinette.

Darth Vader's head-piece is an exaggerated Nazi helmet and the wicked Imperial commanders wear bottle-green uniforms reminiscent of Nazi and Communist ones, while the rebel pilots wear loose orange flying-suits rather like American carrier pilots.

Overarchingly, the belief-system of *Star Wars*, made explicit at the conclusion of *Return of the Jedi*, is optimistic: despite all odds, when even the best efforts of the best seem to have failed, things will come eucatastrophicly right in the end. The past gives meaning to the present and future. The fate of the individual soul is desperately important, and the efforts Luke Skywalker puts into saving the "lost" soul of Darth Vader are not in vain. There seems to be some sort of supernatural standard by which judgements or morality and value may be made. In the final redemption of Darth Vader one sees a suggestion of Divine Mercy. When, as the evil Emperor's fortress collapses around them in *Return of the Jedi*, Luke tells him: "I'll save you," Vader, who knows he is dying, replies in a now calm and peaceful voice: "You already have."

This Western milieu of values and attitudes is also true of the series of spin-off novels and comics, which are for the most part ordinary adventure stories in which there is some kind of eventual triumph for the good side.

The implications of the *Alien* films, on the other hand, are almost total pessimism and nihilism: humans, who anyway seem to be motivated principally by greed and treachery, are defeated and destroyed by the mindless, ferocious Aliens who exist only to kill and breed — the Aliens in this *Weltenschauung* are, in fact, humanity taken to its logical conclusion and stripped of the illusions of conscience, ethics and free will (How predatory creatures at once so ferocious, indestructible and fecund manage to survive at all without eating out their supply of prey-animals is not explained). One of the Alien comic-stories explains that even the standard of morality which judges the Aliens horrifying is a local human illusion. The "artistic" driving force behind them is sensation for its own sake.

The films' sets tend to look like decayed factories in East Germany, and the first even manages a sort of dirty rain inside a space-ship. Sigorney Weaver in one remarkable interview actually spoke of preserving their "values," which was about the first time I have heard nihilism, sadism and industrial filth so described. Certainly, to anyone sensitive to atmosphere, they succeed in being unhappy and depressing.

Any bravery the humans show in attempting to resist the Aliens is not inspired by an abstract concept of nobility but is simply an attempt at self-preservation. There is tactical co-operation if there is an obvious need for it, but almost no real altruism.

The heroine Ripley's attempts to save the little girl Newt in *Aliens* (the second film) are, it seems, simply the products of a mother-instinct, pre-determined and not necessarily more moral or ethical than the Queen Alien's concern for her eggs, and are ultimately futile anyway. All does not come right in the end.

While Ripley may seem an icon of Feminist liberation, pursuing Aliens with a flame-thrower after her male and female colleagues have been torn to pieces or otherwise made away with, and, in the very dramatic showdown with the Queen in *Aliens*, appearing John Wayne-like and clumping out in a power-operated Waldo outfit, there is little indication that she has any moral choice in the matter — she is simply a puppet of circumstances who has seen the odds and the possible courses of action for the best chance of survival more clearly than the others. Anyway she, like the others, including the other females, perishes in lurid circumstances sooner or later. The universe of the Aliens, unlike that of *Star Wars*, has all its implications against the Judeo-Christian notion that each individual creature is precious to a benevolent God. It is, in fact, not far from a species of Satanism.

One of the few who behaves impressively in *Aliens* is Bishop, who is not a human but a programmed robot. The Aliens are born out of their larval stage by killing their hosts and the nature of life is to destroy. It is Darwinism stripped down to nothing but *The Selfish Gene* and there is certainly no room for religious or other values in the process. Indeed, the point is specifically made in the book of the film *Aliens* that the humans are at least no better and possibly worse than the Aliens, who being mindless are at least incapable of conscious betrayal (this possibly involves a logical fallacy but there is no space to explore it here).

Any victories by the humans, as at the end of the second film when the Queen Alien is destroyed and the Alien hive has been nuked, are illusory. The Queen has laid eggs which in the next film hatch and destroy the human survivors including the appealing and freshly washed-and-brushed little girl Newt.

The mindless Aliens are not, unlike Darth Vader or Jabba the Hutt, originally good creatures that have been corrupted, but the expression of an intrinsically nihilistic and destructive universe. The *Alien* publishing industry reflects this *Weltenschauung*. As well as a set of books there are now a number of *Alien* comics. These are sometimes very impressively drawn, with far more conceptually-sophisticated story-lines than are now to be found in many more conventionally literary works.

While *Star Wars* aimed to thrill, the *Alien* films worked to cause terror and propagate nihilism. The Aliens, at least the first time one is seen, are nightmarish creatures, and every type of manipulative device, such as exaggerated heart-heats on the soundtrack, is employed to accentuate the terror.

Where *Star Wars* is in general socially conservative, the *Alien* trilogy and the associated books and "graphic novels" are in a sense Left-wing, though not in a hopeful or idealistic way: Capitalism rules and is evil, indeed the rapacious natures of Capitalism and of the Aliens merge as a statement about the nature of the universe. Where *Star Wars* has moments of contemplation (as when Luke gazes out at the double-sunset of Tattooine) and even a sort of poetry (as in Obe-Wan's admonition that: "The Jundland wastes are not to be travelled lightly"), *Aliens* presents a series of shlock sensations, dependent entirely on horror, destruction and terror.

The crew of the space-tug in *Alien*, the colonists and marines in *Aliens*, and the mine-caretakers in *Alien III* are all sacrificed to revolting deaths by the ruthless "company" which wants Aliens for its "bioweapons division", and it is prepared to put risk all Earth by bringing specimens back. It is taken for granted that the Company will lie, murder and rape the universe and is driven by nothing but profits.

Politics, like idealism, is futile, and humans are the victims of infinite malign forces. Presumably activity creates an illusion of free-will, and if the political background of *Star Wars* looks to Burke, that of the *Alien* films looks, perhaps, to a combination of Sartre and the Marquis de Sade. It is the stifling atmosphere of *No Exist*, with the addition of terror, teeth in the dark, slime and gouts of blood and entrails. A few years ago some of the Alien comics would have been banned. In one a character is expected to copulate with his mother whose arms and legs have previously been torn off by Aliens. All is shown in high (of course coloured) visual detail — with, for example, a naked bone protruding from the stump of the mother's left shoulder, the other shoulder being an empty socket. In what turns out to be an uncharacteristic burst of compassion he strangles her. This gives the graphic artist further opportunities. This, be it noted, is a comic — or rather a "graphic novel" — targeted at children or teenagers and sold without any restrictions on the age of the buyers. As mentioned above, the drawings are done with very considerable skill.

This is only one of a series of similar themes and incidents, and part of a constant tone. A character who has been tortured by the Aliens (one sees in some detail the bloody cavity where his sexual organs have been torn off, apparently the start rather than the end of his problems), does not merely scream, but screams till his vocal chords are shredded, after which he continues to make a noise "like a goose. Hour after hour after hour."

Innocence and goodness are occasionally portrayed (not unskil-
fully) simply in order to be betrayed and annihilated.

Sexual sadism is not so much a theme as, in combination
with nihilism, the series' *raison d'être*. This part of the Alien industry is also Feminist in that women are shown to come apart
at least as easily and spectacularly as men. A "sex-synth", a
human-appearing robot programmed to sexually service a space-
ship's crew, named Judith, (who is also a botanist, perhaps in
graceful tribute to *ET*), attempts to defend her patients from the
Aliens, and no detail of her subsequent dismembering is omit-
ted. Human prisoners of the Aliens, hung up and partially dis-
membered while being kept alive for breeding, are force-fed by
the Aliens (from their mouths) with the entrails of the decaying,
liquifying corpses of their predecessors. There would be no point
in rebuking the authors of these works for bad taste or sadism
when, for example, the coda to one comic apologises for the
relative absence of "chest-bursters". The Communist Party writers who, in the 1950s, railed at American comics as decadent
and degrading, didn't know the half of it. It is, as a novelist
friend of mine commented, like a pillow-book from the court of
Caligula.

If C S Lewis used the "Narnia" stories to subtly introduce
children to Christian values under the guise of fantasy, the equivalent direction is equally unambiguous here.

In one sense this may seem far from the cultural politics of
Britain at the end of the Twentieth Century. In another it does
not. Quite apart from, and in addition to, the romantic revolutionary and Rousseauian notion expressed by Wordsworth that
"Heaven lies about us in our infancy," young people, and in
some cases like Pol Pot's Cambodia and the China of the Great
Proletarian Cultural Revolution, literally children, can be vital
shock-troops: unless educated in a special way they have little if
any feeling for traditions and values, little if any feelings of compassion and humanity or of informed conscience or judgement.
Their mobilisation is an important part of cultural war.

Chapter 8 New Nihilism

The aimed-for culture of New Britain inevitably points towards desolation. This is a necessary part of the erasure of the past. It is a landscape from which everything positive, cherished or in the deepest sense reassuring has been removed. The destruction of tradition, and its replacement by a succession of fashions, means the spiritual impoverishment of existence. Along with a sense or loss and ruin, it is also one of the causes of a pervasive sense of anxiety. This is to some extent the case in any period of social and cultural change, but the matter of degree is important.

It was only really after the end of the Cold War that a condition called "Twentieth Century Blues" came to be identified, something akin to mass clinical depression, a feeling that — for no very easily-defined reason — life was out of control and had become too complex to cope with. It was a feeling of *angst* qualitatively different from that experienced when living with the possibility of Nuclear holocaust. Indeed it was only in this period that the phrase "unable to cope" began to be widely used and understood as referring to a widespread and inevitable condition. This is plainly a cultural as well as a medical phenomenon.

It is true and obvious that in many circumstances social and cultural change may be accompanied by positive senses of renewal and purpose. However, there are indications that in very large parts of the contemporary cultural revolution this has not been the case. Despite localised exceptions, crime, drug-abuse, divorce, suicide and other indicators of profound social unhappiness have continued to increase, at least in advanced societies where reliable statistics were kept. It seems in retrospect that a great dissolving of established values had begun in the 1960s — a process of dissolution which shows no sign of stopping.

J M Roberts, vice-chancellor of the University of Southampton and 25 years a Fellow of Merton College, wrote in 1985:

> Age-old hatreds and bitternesses have not been exorcised; new ones have appeared ... old faith in the technological dynamic is questioned ... technical prowess no longer seems to point so obviously and unambiguously as once it did to a cheery future ... Citizens of the great North American republic, in a more optimistic age 'the world's last, best hope' now dabble in oriental religion, mysticism and the fads of those who reject individualism ...[152]

Despite — or because of — material prosperity and a level of international peace and security unknown since 1914, there seemed to be abroad a grim sense that things were going to get worse. The Queen said in 1997: "The world is changing too fast ... At least for us older ones." In the context, this was an acknowledgement of an apparently out-of-control process and widespread bewilderment and distress in all age-groups and all parts of society. In the Britain of New Labour a short and somewhat trite collection of sayings, *The Little Book of Calm*, remained on the best-seller list for week after week, indicating that many people felt a desperate need for an instruction-manual on peace of mind. Religion had once made a promise of bliss that transcended all Earthly happiness, but the churches were nearly empty. Writing in *Prospect* in December, 1997, Marion McGilvary stated, not as any kind of original supposition but as an obvious and taken-for-granted fact, that:

Throughout the developed world we are generally unhappier than we were 30 years ago.

In its Christmas leader published on 21 December, 1997, the *Sunday Telegraph* pronounced:

> Few societies have been as riven with self-doubt and ethical uncertainty as our own, yet we live in much the most prosperous civilisation that has ever existed. Wealth is more widely distributed, health better and education more generally available than at any time in human history. In spite of this — or perhaps because of it — ours seems to be an instinctively anxious rather than an instinctively optimistic age ... It is as though, stripped of the need to hope, we have forgotten how to do so ...

Its stablemate, the *Daily Telegraph*, claimed in its Christmas Eve leader of 24 December, 1997, of the Millennium Dome:

> Nothing is inside ...This is true not only as a physical fact — the building work has not yet been done — but also true as a metaphor. The Dome is empty. It stands for the vacuum of a civilisation that has lost understanding of what makes it civilised.

Writing in the same paper on 31 December, 1997, Boris Johnson stated:

> Enormous prosperity, spiritual emptiness and the approaching millennium have encouraged a free-floating angst.

This unhappiness was perhaps most notable and obvious in the profoundly negative and nihilistic slant to both high and popular culture, to art, literature, music, to fashions, to the media, and to many aspects of education. Healthy people are not nihilistic in behaviour and this torrent of nihilism seemed profoundly abnormal.

One example of what had happened might be seen in the
weekend magazine of the *Daily Telegraph* of 2 May, 1998. I have
chosen this example because the *Telegraph* is the *most conservative*
and also the *least sleazy and nihilistic* major British newspaper.

The cover, in appropriate black and white, black predomi-
nating, showing an apparently alienated female face, headlined
its major story as SEX DRINK AND FRANCIS BACON. Its
features, listed on the following page, were as follows:

Bringing home the Bacon: The furore over the controversial
new film on the life and lust of Francis Bacon;

Special Agent: The rise and rise of Britain's coolest modelling
agency;

Cave's New World: How Nick Cave turned from raging rocker
to literary sensation;

Life After Life: Jailed for killing her abusive lover, Emma
Humphries now faces a new struggle: coping with freedom;

Top of the Mops: A chance for young dancers to strut their
stuff;

It was morning in Oxford when I began to read this. After a
time I threw it away and my wife and I went down to a cafe
beside a swift-rushing river that sparkled in the sun. There were
flowers and peacocks and people laughing. I was struck again
by the contrast between a media culture — not now an
underground culture — of misery and ugliness and the beauty
and wonder that was available in the world. How easily that
beautiful river could be polluted by toxic sludge as our culture
and minds were being polluted by its intellectual equivalent!
That afternoon we wandered through the Ashmolean Museum
drinking in some of the glories of Greece and Egypt and Rome,
the strength and beauty and wisdom which those poor and

primitive societies had yet been able to celebrate.

There seemed, at a time when opportunities had never been brighter, and the skies should never have been more blue, a perverse, willed turning-away from happiness, that had no obvious social or economic cause, but which came from some region deeper and harder to define. The retailing of negativity and despair in all manner of art, entertainment, literature and lifestyle had become a great vested industry, and a partly self-fulfilling prophecy.

Writing in *The Spectator* of 9 May, 1998, theatre critic Harry Eyres claimed that:

> At moments recently it has seemed that the theatrical powers-that-be ... have decided that audiences' attention can only be held by acts of ever grosser lewdness, pointless violence or self-destruction.

What made this observation particularly notable was that he went on to uphold the bleak, hopelessly pessimistic works of Samuel Beckett as a positive and encouraging contrast!

A few years earlier, the *Daily Telegraph's* columnist "Peter Simple" (Michael Wharton) had written:

> Hywall Rowlands, a young father, drugged his beloved six-year-old daughter and then dropped her off the Severn Bridge. He told police: "I had to do it. There was no future for her in this world, with drug addiction, prostitution and nuclear power. What a terrible world to bring up children."

> In a letter to his wife he asked her to forgive him for what he had done. "I could not bear to think of her being left alone in the world after we had gone."

> At his trial the judge sentenced him to seven years' jail, saying that though previously "an admirable husband and father", he was a continuing risk to himself, his wife and possibly others, and that no hospital could provide adequate security.

This is one of the saddest things I have ever heard ...

What drove him to it? The world has always been terrible. Isn't it possible the continual projection of terrifying images of death and destruction in the "media", particularly on television, the continual harping on evil which is itself a cause of evil, may have had a lot to do with it?

Those who set out — it has become a monstrous kind of profession — to destroy all hope in this world while offering no hope in any world beyond, have a lot to answer for. Those who assiduously foment despair are a far greater danger to others than this despairing and most pitiable man.

Hywell Rowlands was by no means the last to so react to the relentless bombardment of negativity. It was, for example, reported from Australia on 1 July, 1997, that a Tasmanian poet, Peter Shoebridge, killed his four children and then himself, writing "Would it be right to bring children up in such a world?"

Previous societies have broadly agreed that stories which tell of, and teach, virtue, whose characters are heroes and exemplars, are stories which benefit both society and the individual who is affected by them, and which ought to be encouraged. A clergyman, the Rev Marcus Morris, founded the *Eagle* comic, which first appeared in 1950, quite deliberately to publish adventure stories that put forward ethics of positive values without rubbing juvenile noses in them.[153] Its heroes were honourable, brave, self-sacrificing and did not regard God and Christianity as irrelevant. This religious element was not at all heavy-handed. Thus a Space-explorer marooned on a distant planet counted a Bible among his possessions and stopped to pray for a dead comrade, and along with the Space, Foreign-Legion, sea, Wild West and detective stories, there were major serialisations of the lives of Christ, Saint Paul and secular historical figures who might be taken as inspirational and exemplary, all meticulously researched and illustrated with what was often extraordinary art and skill.

Eagle was consciously non-racist and in one of the very first stories, published in the early 1950s, long before integration in American schools, a space-station in the early Twenty-First Century had black as well as white crew-members, all brave and dedicated. The leading scientist was a woman. None of this was done obtrusively or in pandering to any political correctness. It simply suggested that in the better, exciting, optimistic world of the future that was how things would be. It was in considerable contrast to many other British comics then and practically all since which have simply pandered to a perceived prolefeed culture of sports (increasingly soccer rather than cricket or rugby union), World War II (at least until recently) and general social resentment.

Eagle, incidentally, was hugely successful until its format was changed under new and self-destructive management in the 1960s when it also lost its resident genius Frank Hampson, creator of the Space-pilot hero Colonel Dan Dare and his Sancho Panza, Spaceman Digby (It was depressing to see what happened to *Eagle* after this as it gave away its unique qualities and sank into the general prolefeed morass and eventual merciful oblivion). It was sometimes claimed that *Eagle* had been a victim of changing times. In fact it had been a victim of its new proprietors' absence of greatness and purpose.

J R R Tolkien's *The Lord of The Rings* was also infused with a commitment to positive values, as more recently were *Star Wars* as described above, and *Star Trek*. The *Thomas the Tank Engine* stories depicted a sunny, innocent world. These were all phenomenally successful. It is generally easier to write about Nihilism, despair and negativity than hope and affirmation, but it is not always more profitable. It is commonplace that *The Lord of The Rings* and *Star Wars* are the re-telling of timeless myths and — plainly in the case of *The Lord of The Rings* but I would argue in *Star Wars* as well — myths set in a specifically Christian framework.[154]

It is still adventure stories with some kind of heroic and positive themes that are reliably good cinema box-office. The same is largely true of books, both adult and juvenile. In a poll of their favourite books commissioned by the BBC's *Bookworm* magazine, of 10,000 children's book readers, *Junk* failed to "make it",[155] being still eclipsed by the positive, affirmative works of C S Lewis, J R R Tolkien, *Swallows and Amazons* and classics like *The Wind in the Willows*. It was a result which drove the literary editor of the London *Observer*, Robert McCrum, to rail against "this bunch of dead authors", and to suggest that those polled may have been "brainwashed by a middle-class education establishment." He continued that the poll result was "strangely at variance with the world as it actually is" and asked somewhat plaintively: "Is it just escapism from the troubling and violent confusions of the alternative available narratives on film and television ..."[156]

The kind of innocent, values-affirming stories thought to be of a previous generation (the *Swallows and Amazons* stories, of which more below, have been made a sort of anti-icon of these) are held up for ridicule and denigration. The following from a major newspaper is typical:

> Danny is one of the least pleasant protagonists in [young adult] fiction ... it is, of course, no criticism to say that these charac-ters are not the admirable kind of heroes that readers of my generation found in *Swallows and Amazons* ... Given what Danny does in this novel, it would be a moral challenge if he were "nice" ... Young people also face questions of racism, sexuality, drugs, family dysfunction, homelessness. And if the present world is bleak, compared to the paradise of the baby-boomer's adolescence, the future must be alarming to any thinking kid. From HIV/AIDS to the hole in the ozone layer, there doesn't seem much hope of a happy ending. Young [people] wouldn't be suiciding so frequently if life were good ...[157]

What planet have you been living on, Lady? one might ask the learned author of this piece. The "Baby-boomers" grew up not in a paradise but in a world that lived in the shadow of nuclear

holocaust, a world where living standards were in material terms
far lower than today in practically every developed society and
where social welfare was far scantier and sometimes non-exist-
ent.

Practically every family had been maimed by the Second
World War. The recently-opened Nazi extermination camps
cried out what Man was capable of. The Soviet Gulags were in
operation from East Europe to the Arctic. George Orwell wrote
1984 from the stuff of life about him on every side. In Britain it
was common for families to live in caravans on bomb-sites and
food-rationing lasted into the 1950s. (It was no coincidence that
children's books by Enid Blyton and others in the 1950s were
filled with descriptions of food.) Refugees and concentration-
camp survivors still wandered between the barbed wire. Even
relatively affluent Western countries still at various times had
forms of conscription. The Soviet Union claimed possession of a
100-megaton Hydrogen Bomb. Some paradise! some might say.
With qualifications for his opinion, Albert Speer in a Spandau
prison cell would lie sleepless with horror at the news of the
Sputnik which seemed to him to presage the next and final war.

Medical treatments in the 1940s and 1950s were primitive
compared to today, more painful and less effective,[158] and a great
many more jobs, both in employment and domestically, were
dull, futile, soul-destroying (and sometimes body-destroying) toil.
Many jobs which later disappeared in old industries were jobs
which few people in affluent countries would be prepared to
take today (how satisfactory, except for the Epsilon-minus semi-
morons of *Brave New World*, is a life spent as a lift-driver?). There
were then fewer opportunities to invest or accumulate money,
for self-education or for other self-improvement, and a far smaller
proportion of people were property or share-owners.

By the 1990s consumer goods were incomparably better.
Opportunities for holidays, travel and luxuries formerly available
only to the rich had come well within the reach of practically all
ordinary working people. Indeed the whole travel, leisure,

entertainment and service industry generally had exploded. Tertiary education had become open to anyone with ability (and many without) who seriously wanted it.

If people were less unhappy in the 1940s and 1950s (and I myself, a baby-boomer in Australia, am able to remember a more stable, happy and moral society), it was surely because they were not bombarded with messages and presumptions of hopelessness, breakdown, misery and despair of which both the above piece of journalism and the book it celebrates are examples. Some paradise!

And yet in a way it was. There was courage, honour, hopefulness, and, as I recall the world around me when I was growing up, despite many problems and even tragedies there was a vast lack of cultural despair or even self-pity. Did the fact that so many of our parents and our teachers were ex-service personnel have anything to do with this, I wonder? Juvenile suicide was absolutely unheard of in my, and I think every other, socio-economic bracket.

The piece quoted above is a good example of a self-fulfilling prophecy: if nihilism, despair and hopelessness among young people are not widespread, given this kind of relentless propaganda, they will soon become more so. Much of the media and the publishing-entertainment industries have so departed from elementary moral sense today that they appear utterly indifferent to the fact — emphasised to me many years ago as a cadet reporter on a long-vanished newspaper with a moral conscience — that to shock-horror expose certain things is often functionally the same as promoting them. Of course, exactly the same thing is true in literature and probably particularly true in juvenile literature.

It is probable that Richmal Crompton's largely pre-war *William* stories, about a naughty 11-year-old English boy, had a much healthier attitude than modern "realistic" work when they occasionally mentioned drug-abuse: that is, that it was not tragic but ridiculous. In the *William* stories the occasionally-referred-to "Drug Maniacs" were not existential heroes or heroines living at the extremes of experience but people to laugh at. It was probably a much more effective deterrent to young people from getting involved in a drug-culture than anything today.

Those much-despised *Swallows and Amazons* stories (actually written in the '20s and '30s and still very popular today), and apparently, according to a number of modern commentators, about a false paradise, were actually about children, principally the Walker family who, in the first book, counted themselves lucky to be allowed to borrow a sailing dinghy to go camping on a lake-island, whose mother (their father was away in the Navy) helped them sew their own tents, and who got the very modest presents of pocket electric torches for a birthday.

Few of the "despairing" generation of the '90s would have been content with so little. It is worth noting that the "drugs, family dysfunction, homelessness" listed above, as well as boredom and hopelessness, are to a large extent the result not of destructive natural forces or malevolent enemies, but of lifestyle choices. What made the children of the stories — and indeed probably the real children who read the stories — different and allegedly unreal was that they were not made to resonate with a culture of despair. It was revealed in dialogue and action in *Swallowdale*, the second book (and just hinted at in the first) that the Walker's friends and rivals the Blackett girls (the Amazons) and their mother were bravely coping with, and refusing to give in to, the deep emotional wound of the loss of their father, presumably in World War I (Nancy just remembers him, Peggy doesn't. He may have died of wounds after the war). One also realises, gradually, that the Blacketts are in reduced circumstances and can barely afford to maintain their house at Beckfoot — it can only be redecorated because of the windfall success of their uncle's book.

Indeed, the stories were largely not about idealised nuclear families, but families making the best of things. The various Walker children displayed deep insecurities, and the Callums, who entered the series later, were practically freaks. The stories (it is no coincidence that they seem to have appealed strongly to children with difficult childhoods) were about being happy in spite of the odds and the malignancies of fate.

There are other things about the *Swallows and Amazons* and *William* stories which in the modern cultural context seen significant: reading them reminds one how far the modern proletarianisation of culture has gone in terms of an attack on individualism, and how far it appears to have advanced towards the mass-culture Aldous Huxley warned against in *Brave New World*. The Swallows and Amazons and William, part of a long tradition of children's literature, are the heroes of their own fantasy adventures — it is William's defining characteristic that he assumes the role of Hero in any adventure he imagines or is placed in. They are not "fans" of rock-stars or sports-stars, or of football teams. The boys in these adventures may kick a football around with friends occasionally, but it is a very small part of their lives and something they enjoy on their own terms. They are anything but the modern processed and manipulated mass-consumers of a divide-and-drool football cult (if William and the Outlaws follow organised spectator sport they tend to show more interest in cricket, obviously still a more individualistic game). They are not "fans", nor do they have any of that term's connotations of passive, manipulated, proletarian consumerism.

The closest modern equivalent of William is not British at all but the American Calvin of *Calvin and Hobbes*, a naughty six-year-old individualist who loathes mass-participation sports and prefers to create his own imaginary worlds in the company of a toy tiger. A few years ago Calvin would have seemed a quintessentially British figure — the lone boy hero, a tradition encompassing not only William but Jim Hawkins and Ransome's John Walker who has dreamed of being a sailor and is suddenly forced to take command of a yacht drifting across the North Sea.

It would in fact be hard to imagine a greater gap between

notions of sport as light-hearted and enjoyable individual achievement and what it has overwhelmingly become — an industry
devoid of spontaneity, fun, good-fellowship or even, for most of
its passive audience, the physical benefits of exercise. However
useful it may now be as a social opiate and money-generator —
its obvious purposes — it has very little to do with happiness
and friendship in the sense that was previously important.[159]
Today, as senior sports writer Paul Hayward has put it:

> Soccer provides the perfect synthesis between pop, sport and
> the cat-walk. Its modern icons date Spice Girls and dye their
> hair a la David Beckenham. Anthony Clare, the psychologist,
> has written that Britain's gleaming all-seater stadiums are the
> new cathedrals ... young people ... are susceptible to the daily
> bombardment of World Cup imagery on cereal boxes and tow-
> els. To turn one's back on the country's national obsession in
> to make a cultural outcast of oneself.[160]

There are other significant things about the *William* stories:
William and his friends call themselves the Outlaws and many
of their games revolve around Red Indians (presumably now
Native Americans), pirates and smugglers. Their *real* criminality
extends to occasionally robbing orchards and trespassing in
woods. It seems to William that he has "drunk from ecstasy's
very font" when he is playing in the woods in a bear-suit and
surprises another small boy who flees in terror. The Outlaws
alter the sign above the shop of an unfriendly barber from
"Theobald Hairdresser" to "The bald Hairdresser." William
would never lie or do anything in conflict with what was then
the generally socially-accepted code of honour.

Their awareness of sexuality — if I can use such a term here
without being totally grotesque — is largely expressed in dis-
trust of girls tempered by ambitions to impress them if they are
pretty. I wrote "William and his friends" rather than "William
and his gang" because of the obvious gulf between this and real

juvenile gangs today. When the *William* stories were first published, however, they were *not* seen either by children or adults
as idealised fantasies or nostalgic depictions of a golden age of
childhood which had never in fact existed. Children are dis-
cerning critics of stories of childhood, and I know that when I
first encountered William in the 1950s neither I nor any of the
other children I knew who read them thought of them as unreal. We were, of course, aware that they were fiction and not
literally true, but they seemed to us — and to me they seem still
— true to the spirit of the experience of childhood then in a way
that, for example, we knew the interminable Greyfriars-clone
school stories were not. We did not do exactly the things William
and the Outlaws did, but our real adventures were in recognis-
ably the same sort of world as their real adventures: catching
tadpoles, stealing fruit from trees, thrilling at the visits of cir-
cuses ... The contrast between the atmosphere of that world
and the world to which children are exposed today is stark and
terrible, the more so because these stories were not written long
ago. The last ones had themes from the space-age.

It may be objected that these stories are simply propaganda
for the middle-class. William's family is plainly comfortably
middle-class and in the pre-war stories even has servants. It is
impossible to know how much these stories were written with
deliberate didactic intent but their politics to an adult readers
are obviously and unashamedly conservative with a tinge of
anarchy — at least one of them has a plot explicitly refuting
Communism. This however is not the point, or rather if it is the
point, it is no point in their disfavour. The *William* stories were
read by children of all classes, and provided an idea that a world
of gentleness, decency, good behaviour and innocence was not
only possible but normal. They were high among the arche-
typal children's books which, in Britain, played a major role in
upholding civilised values.

To illustrate the modern contrast, here is piece of cultural
barbarism from a Sunday newspaper (in this case an Australian

one, but illustrative of the point):

> It is difficult to persuade teenagers to read. It's often a matter of convincing them that the books won't up and grab them by the throat.

> As a teacher, I find myself launching into spiels about how it's an achievement to read a novel [!] and that they'll be justifiably proud on turning the final page ...

> Publishers have become increasingly aware that kids do judge a book by its cover initially, that graphics must have the sharp visual impact of music video clips or kids won't bother. The pace, too, has to be fast, with 3D characters, up-to-date vernacular and situations they can believe in.

> [This] is a new series on the market for young adults ... in sync with teenagers, unafraid to confront issues like suicide, family breakdown and desolation but challenging readers to hope and strive for self-realisation in the face of it all. ...

That is the real thing, the authentic voice of Caliban, a yawp that can't be counterfeited. Imagine the great writers of previous ages claiming, as a positive thing, that books would, while apparently presenting "suicide, family breakdown and desolation" as a normal part of childhood (they aren't, or at least not yet), help children strive for "self-realisation", whatever that means, in the face of it all!

This seems to be trying to replicate the common situation of the chronic neurotic whose thoughts endlessly revolve around his or her desolation. This may merge into the clinical depression in which selfhood becomes a black horror.

I remember one of the very first books my parents read me, when I was not a teenager but a pre-school infant. It was the story of a cicada grub who lived in the dark underground knowing that one day he would climb up into the sky and air "a bright, warm, wonderful place." Even when I was a five-year-old the symbolism spoke to me: there was a world awaiting me that could be full of wonder and opportunity.

Somewhat later we studied *Lord of the Flies* for our School Leaving exam text and at my school our English master led us on to other Golding works including *The Inheritors* and *Pincher Martin*. These led, I think, to a better understanding of evil, very different to a *Weltenschauung* immersed in and bounded by Nihilism, self-obsession and despair. Further, by that time we were in our late teens and with luck had other furniture in our heads as well.

In 1997 playwright and columnist Keith Waterhouse (author of, among other things, the famous 1960s drama and film *Billy Liar* and *Jubb*, the somewhat yuckily realistic story of a member of the dirty-raincoat brigade), commented of the entries that year that they dealt with:

> Heroin addiction, arson, and a bullied heroine who dies on the operating table while undergoing surgery for sticking-out ears ... not having read any of the short-listed stories, and having no intention of doing so, I express no view on their suitability ... except to observe that it does seem to be the tendency of modern juvenile fiction to rub children's noses in real life.

The same point was made, although with some exultation and very typical aggressiveness, by British children's author John Marsden, who was reported as saying: "Anyone who doesn't want to confront the bleak images of sex and violence he portrays in some of his fiction may as well stick to reading Enid Blyton for the rest of their [*sic*] lives."

Children, according to Mr Marsden, needed fiction that: "tells it like it is ... in a world where we're constantly being presented with images of bleakness, it would be very dishonest if fiction writers ignored that."

A few weeks after this interview was published, the 1997 Carnegie Medal Winner for children's book of the year was announced (*Swallows and Amazons* had been the first winner when the medal was instituted). According to one newspaper:

> A book about heroin addiction, under-age sex and prostitution has won Britain's Carnegie Medal, the children's equivalent of the Booker Prize.

This book, *Junk*, by 43-year-old Melvin Burgess, was praised by the judging panel for its ground-breaking approach, realistic social commentary and gripping drama.

Set in the south-western city of Bristol, the book is about "the drug culture, underground culture, sex, drugs and rock and roll and some runaways who get into it, make some wrong decisions and end up with a heroin problem," Burgess said.

Burgess ... used his acceptance speech to slam the censorship of children's literature.

"There's a nostalgic viewpoint that children should be reading about heroes and heroines, the other sort of heroine, that is, and it should all be escapism ..." Burgess said.

Of course, one answer to this is that posed by C S Lewis a long time ago: "Who hate books about escapism? ... Jailers." It is also a kind of reverse Bowdlerisation, distorting truth to portray the world as darker than it is. Bristol doubtless has many problems. I have seen some of them first-hand. But it is also in many ways a beautiful city, with all sorts of positive opportunities for young people. In that way it is like life. The last time I saw Bristol was on my way to and from Malta, a small and poor society whose people nonetheless seemed happy and full of life and resolution (I don't know what Maltese children read, but most of the ramshackle 1950s buses still have small religious shrines in the drivers' cabs). Quite irrespective of *Junk's* actual plot, the sort of publicity now inevitably surrounding it has consequences of its own. This is not something happening in a vacuum. It is a matter with public sociological and political consequences. Conflict is a usually necessary part of the dramatic storyteller's art, but beyond this it is also possible to see, in the reviews of recent adult novels, an overwhelming preoccupation with evil.

In 1998 it was a strangely alien experience for me to read the American Harry Turtledove's 1993 science-fiction novel about the American Civil War, *The Guns of the South*, and to see, in the author's portraits of Robert E Lee and Abraham Lincoln, loving and moving depictions of *nobility*. It was something I had not seen in any new mainstream novels for a long time. On two successive days I watched on television two black-and-white films from the 1950s, *The Final Test*, concerning an ageing cricketer's last innings, and *Carrington VC*, concerning a court-martialled Army officer who refused to distress his disturbed wife by calling her as a defence witness. Both were concerned as a central issue with that high matter, *Honour*, and both would be unmakable today.

Is it coincidental that another thing notable about this culture is a widespread attack on, or denigration of, perceived symbols of goodness?

A few small examples from Britain make the point. A survey of London clergymen in 1997 revealed that 70% had been either assaulted or threatened with violence, and it was suggested that clergymen be given self-defence classes.[161]

Vachel Lindsay had once written:

Factory windows are always broken.
Other windows are left alone.
No-one throws through the chapel window
The bitter, snarling, derisive stone.[162]

However the *Times* of 30 September, 1997, reported that one in three churches would suffer from some form of arson, theft or vandalism every year. In the same paper it was reported that a 13-year-old girl had been driven to suicide by a gang of teenagers because she was active in the Salvation Army.

The *Daily Telegraph* the same day reported that two 13-year-old girls would make sporting history by becoming the first females to contest an authorised boxing bout in Britain, contrary to the advice of most of the Amateur Boxing Association's medical advisors and the condemnation of the British Medical Association. In March, 1998, the Equal Opportunities Commission enforced the rights of a female professional boxer to pursue her vocation in Britain (a majority of long-term boxers sustained chronic brain damage).

On 10 November, 1997, the *Times* reported that a Mr Ian Erskine, aged 21, had hanged himself at Stratford-on-Avon after constant persecution and tormenting by locals. Two years previously his twin brother, Anthony, had been kicked to death outside his house while attempting to defend his father. Police and neighbours said it was the niceness of the family that made them the target of a hate campaign: "It is thought the perpetrators regarded the hard-working devout Catholic family as snobs ... In the months before Anthony's death all three Erskine sons had been beaten up and their daughter verbally abused. Their hedge had been torched, their car vandalised and their home pelted with eggs, water bombs, stones and bricks." It is, incidentally, quite possible to see some of the much-despised Enid Blyton's work as a morally serious attempt to inculcate virtue and decency. A number of her stories contain some quite powerful lessons against persecuting people who are different. We cannot know exactly what effect such stories have on behaviour, but it is generally agreed that they have some effect and do not exist in a vacuum.

Ian Robertson, former Senior Lecturer in English at the University of Wales, has pointed out:

> The book jacket of Martin Amis's *London Fields* (1989), quotes recommendations from an earlier triumph, *The Rachel Papers*: "Scurrilous, shameless ... ingenious obscenity, loathing, lust, anxiety ... fairly nasty." It tells us much about judgement in the

modern world if a publisher with a very distinguished record thinks "fairly nasty ... ingenious obscenity" are phrases that will lead to sales.[163]

The *Daily Telegraph* published a celebrity interview with the Royal Ballet's principal dancer, Darcey Bussell OBE, who claimed emphatically: "To be told you are nice isn't a compliment." The novelist Joanna Trollope wrote that rural England had become "more sad and savage".[164]

Footnotes

152 J.M. Roberts, *The Triumph of The West* (BBC, 1985), pp 10-11.

153 I had always imagined rather vaguely that Marcus Morris had been wealthy and well-connected. In fact a recent biography by Sally Morris and Jan Hallwood, *Living with Eagles* (The Lutterworth Press, Cambridge, 1998), indicates that he had brought himself to the verge of bankruptcy (and therefore probably defrocking) to start *Eagle*.

154 Colebatch, *Return of the Heroes*

155 It was announced on 11 November 1997, that *Junk* was also shortlisted for the Whitbread Prize. *The Daily Telegraph* commented that it had been described as: "drug tourism for middle class children".

156 Robert McCrum, "McCrum on Children's books", *Observer*, 7 September 1997.

157 Nadia Wheatley, "Age of Discontent", *The Australian's Review of Books*, August 1997.

158 In the 1900s the life-expectancy for *Americans* was less than 50 years.

159 It was no coincidence that the BBC in 1998 was describing football rather than cricket as Britain's "national game".

160 *Daily Telegraph*, 6 June 1998.

161 *Daily Telegraph,* 17 March 1998.
162 "Factory Windows are Always Broken", quoted in Marghanita Laski, *Common Ground* (Carcanet, Manchester), 1989, p.203.
163 "Faking Emotion" in Digby Anderson and Peter Mullen, Editors, *Faking it: The Sentimentalisation of Modern Society* (The Social Affairs Unit, London, 1998), p.131.
164 *Sunday Telegraph,* 1 March 1998.

Chapter 9 Britannia Year Zero?

The title of this chapter, an obvious hearkening-back to the "Year Zero" imposed upon Cambodia when it was liberated by the Pol Pot régime, is not intended to trivialise the memory of that holocaust. I seek to emphasise the radical and unprecedented commitment by large parts of the cultural Nomenklatura and by New Labour to transforming British culture.

We now see there are régimes which are not traditionally totalitarian but nonetheless aim at a totalistic reshaping of their subjects' consciousness. Allied with certain cultural groups, the present "radical centrist" British government is one of these.

Like others who have thought in "Year Zero" terms, these seem driven by an obsessive need to obliterate the past. They seek to remake the culture and to destroy traditions and values, however fundamental they may be, which conflict with this design. This politico/cultural alliance and programme is unprecedented in modern Britain and in the Anglomorph world.

The basic task of conservatism has not changed since the time of Burke: to manage social change so that the human heritage and the human condition in all its aspects is preserved and enhanced rather than diminished and destroyed.

Institutions such as the Conservative Party address or claim to address this in politics and economics at least in theory and with varying degrees of success. The more purely cultural and the immediately human aspects of major social change are a different matter. Continuous and rapid social change, such as has been occurring at a probably unprecedented rate in the Twentieth Century and shows little sign of abating in the Twenty-First, while plainly bringing many benefits, has enormous potential to produce distress, alienation and misery. Doctors can tell of town-planning schemes which cause premature deaths up forcibly uprooting vulnerable people and subjecting them to prolonged and intolerable stress. "Twentieth Century Blues" may be the same thing writ large.

Distress at the decay and loss of loved and cherished institutions and fear of the future may combine to attack the human heart in a pincer-movement. The victims are by no means entirely the older generation set in their ways who regard any change as a sign that the world is going to the dogs: among young people unprecedented rates of suicide, drug-addiction and crime are plain signals of distress and fear. The Dianamania is another indication of those anxieties and disorders at large in society.

In the political area we remember those words of Stewart Steven: "The Blair revolution has barely begun." They may be truer than many today realise. In fact, I believe that many of the signs in Britain today, if not of revolution in the conventional sense of that term, are of profound cultural malaise which is given a particular complexion by the political circumstances of the time. There is something very strange about the attempt to forcibly destroy a country's past traditions and institutions when that country has been one of the most stable and advanced of major nations.

Previously, the command of actual or potential armed force was always implicit in the agenda of conventional Leftism or radicalism. The present nihilistic or quasi-nihilistic cultural climate is a different matter. We cannot imagine armoured divisions or even secret police ideologically dedicated to nihilism as the Red Army and the Wehrmacht were to Communism or National Socialism. Cultural nihilism and its penumbra of post-modernism, moral relativism and what Christopher Booker identified some years ago as neophilia does not need such armed force. It does not even need any precise definition of itself. It does not need a *Communist Manifesto* or *Mein Kampf.* It does not even need Sartre or Foucault for very long — it need only create a certain vague, pervasive climate of opinion, and gain control of certain commanding heights of institutional power and social debate.

The destruction of cultural certainties and landmarks is, I believe, likely to lead to major cultural regression, and further, I believe that in the arts, public life and many other areas signs of that regression are already apparent.

There have been periods of cultural regression before. When the Roman Emperor Constantine found no stone-carver remained in Rome who could create realistic-looking soldiers for monuments and had to take such carvings from earlier works, there were probably Roman wiseacres who pontificated to the effect that this symbolised the decadence of Rome and its approaching demise. They were right.

*   *   *

Cultural collapse may lack the drama of Paris in 1789 or Petrograd in 1917. It has, however, been by no means infrequent. Cultural or systemic collapses of various kinds can be identified in, for example, Italy in the 1920s, Germany in the 1930s, France in 1940, and Yugoslavia and the Soviet Union in the late 1980s, as well as in many other areas outside Europe. While history never repeats itself exactly — it is an important point of this book that the present cultural conditions in Britain are unprecedented — what can be identified in each case is not only or always an economic crisis but also a widespread loss of belief in the structure of society and in the traditions and values that hold that society together. Like an avalanche, cultural or systemic collapses can have consequences far in excess of their apparent causes. And when an avalanche — or a guillotine — falls it falls very fast.

The greatest event of the modern world has been the sudden total collapse of the Soviet Union and the Communist system, at a time when it still commanded immeasurable military and other coercive power. The causes of this collapse will doubtless pre-occupy historians for the foreseeable future and many theories as to its cause will be advanced. However, even when full account is given to the various and complex economic and military factors, the overarching cause remains cultural — the people had finally lost faith in all the institutions of the Communist system. There was no shared structure of feeling, nothing of Burke's moral essence. We see post-Communist Russia today, with enormous potential wealth and a huge fund of scientific and technical education, crippled and part-starving because of the ruin, under Communism, of any system of shared ethics, traditions and values — of that moral essence.

The actually *fall* of civilisations seems to us something that belongs far more to the ancient world than to the modern day — we associate such falls with the ruins of Ancient Egypt, Greece or Rome, or the jungle-grown temples of South America or Cambodia. But if one thinks in terms not of fall but of cultural regression, the idea seems much less archaic and improbable. Like the youth of the British Empire of July, 1914, we have lived so long with general cultural unity and social progress that we have come to take it for granted. Perhaps cultural regression too seems out of the question. And yet it never is. Who, in July, 1914, would have foreseen a war fought by millions year after year in freezing mud with bayonets, trench-knives and poison gas, or, a few years later, slavery and genocide in great European nations? We know all too well the cultural regressions that have occurred under totalitarianism, but totalitarianism is not a necessary pre-condition: Lebanon was one of the most sophisticated countries in the Middle-East but this did not prevent it sinking into apparently interminable civil war and chaos.

It is impossible to guess how far cultural regression or systemic collapse can go. We know it occurred in great and highly-developed civilisations in the ancient world and certainly modernity is no guarantee against it. The Twentieth Century has seen several culturally highly-advanced nations return to barbarism. The rich culture of China did not save it from the madness of the Great Proletarian Cultural Revolution in which millions died and tens or hundreds of millions of lives were gratuitously ruined. The Pol Pot genocide in Cambodia occurred in what was famously a "gentle land".

In the former territory of Yugoslavia, we have seen a modern society completely collapse under pressures which, while real, were not apparently particularly dire and compelling. It is another demonstration of the vulnerability of civilisation once faith in common values has been lost. The Communist systems of Eastern Europe collapsed very quickly once they lost the support of Soviet tanks.

Those East European and former Soviet societies with a strong culture, such as Poland and Hungary, seem to have survived far better, and to have recovered far more quickly, than those which had been "digested" by Communism too long and whose culture, traditions and values had been destroyed. For Russia itself there still seems little evidence of recovery despite its huge resources and assets. In the meantime scores of millions of people are condemned to lives more poor, nasty, brutish and short than they need have been.

* * *

Many a science-fiction story features Aliens who visit Earth at intervals of a few centuries and are awe-struck by the speed of human progress. "They've gone from animal power to space-flight in a hundred years!" the War-Lord of Zwork has a habit of telling his henchman, looking up from a report and twiddling his tentacles in bewilderment. More than one Alien invasion of fiction has come to grief when, expecting to be confronted with the spear-wielding hunter-gatherers which its last spy-probe reported, its landing force is instead assailed with precision-guided laser-beams and nuclear weapons. Certainly there is an element of self-congratulation in these stories.

This is not only true of science-fiction. As human beings we look not only with awe but with a good-deal of self-satisfaction at such achievements of antiquity as the pyramids or the scientific culture which flourished in Alexandria from about 200BC to 100AD and produced such achievements as Hero's steam turbine. We see with amazement a cross-bow mechanism of Han Dynasty China, dated to 147AD, in its case in the Burrell Collection, and think we are looking at a piece of machine-tooled mechanism from the Nineteenth or Twentieth Century, and we feel some complacency at the amazing achievements of the human race.

But, when we consider the pyramids and Hero's turbine and the ancient calculator recovered from a Greek shipwreck, the hydrodynamics of a Viking ship, the philosophic and humanistic achievements of ancient Harrapan civilisation, of Greece, Rome or China, there is another point that strikes us, cold and hard: the question: "Why did it stop?"

For stop it did.

Had the civilisation which built the pyramids so early gone on progressing at anything like the same rate, the sky would not have been any sort of limit. But the knowledge that built the pyramids was not applied to architecture again, let alone improved upon. Indeed, some later pyramids are poor copies of the earlier ones and have collapsed into shapeless mounds. The wonderful Harrapan culture went into rapid decline and vanished about 1500 BC. There are many explanations of why civilisations have fallen — unreliable power sources, loss of faith in oracles, climatic changes, horsemen with swords, lead-poisoning from water-pipes, excessive taxation — but overarching all that we can see is human loss of faith in institutions and loss of shared values.

Nor can purely technical progress be taken for granted. Far from it. Hero's steam turbine had no application, and it was not until the Eighteenth Century that steam was used as motive power.

So many of these ancient achievements were not even maintained, let alone progressed from. We think of the Saxons in Britain gazing in wonder and envy at the ruins of the Roman baths — one of the earliest surviving Anglo-Saxon poems is about these ruined marvels (almost poignantly, the Saxons seems to have known what the baths had been *for*, but knew they were not for them) — and remember how the Fall of Rome once seemed to signify the end of the World. Even in the modern world, while knowledge is almost all retained (as was not the case in the ancient world) we see progress in various directions as being towards plateaux, which are often reached quite quickly.

Robert Zubrin, an astronautic engineer, writing in *The Case for Mars*, published in 1996, invited readers to compare the period 1966-1996 with the preceding thirty years and with the thirty before that. He argues that during the period 1906-1936 the world was revolutionised by electrification, telephones, radio, motor cars, aviation, motion pictures etc (some of these things had certainly come into existence earlier but were developed enormously beyond rudimentary forms only after 1906). Then in 1936-66 came communications satellites, interplanetary spacecraft, computers, television, antibiotics, nuclear power and major improvements in aircraft. He continued:

> Compared to these changes, the technological innovation from 1966 to the present seem insignificant. Immense changes should have occurred during the period but did not. Had we been following the pervious sixty years technological trajectory, we would today have videotelephones, solar-powered cars, maglev (magnetic levitation) trains, fusion reactors, hypersonic intercontinental travel, reliable and inexpensive transportation in

Earth orbit, undersea cities, open-sea mariculture, and human
settlements on the Moon and Mars. Instead, today we see important technological developments, such as nuclear power and
biotechnology, being blocked or enmeshed in controversy —
we are slowing down.

It is, of course, possible to disagree with this. It may properly be
claimed that biotechnology, for example, should be approached
with the greatest caution. Further, it may be argued that there
have been major developments, but in unforeseen areas, such as
Information Technology. However Zubrin makes a case.
Progress is not inevitable.

*   *   *

It is one of the great lessons of recent history that material wealth
does *not* guarantee national prosperity or decent living. North-
Western Europe, Japan and Singapore are poor in natural resources but prosperous; Mexico, the Congo and Brazil are
materially rich but poverty-stricken. It is *culture* and human resources, nothing else, that in the long run makes prosperity, happiness and life itself possible.

Could British society undergo a systemic collapse? Perhaps
some of the worst housing estates might be said to be in a state
of systemic collapse already. The conditions of some prisons and
some aspects of mental health care seem to be stuck at, or regressing to, a state which should be utterly intolerable in a civilised country in the modern world. Perhaps a more sensible
question might be: "When does a cultural malaise become a
collapse?" What may be seen is a general relationship between
cultural malaise and systemic collapse.

The renowned science-fiction author Nigel Kneale, long after
his three brilliantly original *Quatermass* stories, in which Britain
was threatened by varieties of Alien invasion, published a fourth,
in many ways the bleakest, in which British society had collapsed

almost imperceptibly from within. In Central London a
Government still held some sketchy authority as well as its own
comforts and privileges, and there was still a fair amount of
official traffic in the streets around Whitehall, but the rest of the
city was a jungle of savage warring gangs, vast libraries of books
were being sold at gimcrack markets as fuel, old people starved
and died, and bewildered children wandered about the ancient
stone circles of the countryside, hoping to be mystically
transported to some distant, paradisical planet.

Systemic or cultural collapse may of course take a far less
apocalyptic form. It may merely mean stunted, impoverished
lives in a milieu of dreary boredom from which hope, beauty or
senses of adventure or of the numinous have been excluded —
limbo or one of the cool outer circles of Hell rather than the
Inferno or the ice of the Pit.

Cultural artefacts may make a difference here. There are
children on crime and drugs-ridden housing estates at this moment to whose lives it may make a profound difference if they
are given access to a book or film like *Junk* or *Trainspotting* or to
tales of King Arthur or *The Lord of The Rings*. Some cultural
alternatives and choices are obvious: Mozart or Oasis? *Star Wars*
or *Aliens*? Turner or Damien Hirst? Performance poetry or *The
Ballad of the White Horse*? Some cultural differences are less obvious but real: busty girls in the context of the *Sun* or in the context of the *Carry On* Films, memorably described by the Australian
poet Peter Kocan as "a brand of humour that can only work
because it presupposes decency"? See these choices as reflect-
ing not only the fates of individuals but the predominant cultural patterns of an entire society and something of the shape of
modern cultural conflict can perhaps be discerned.

The world is already full of broken-backed societies whose
political institutions and culture climates combine to create not
the killing fields but simply dull, pervasive unhappiness, frustra-
tion, and anxiety. However history never repeats itself exactly
and we can be sure future cultural collapses will be different to

past ones.

We can, however, see certain recurrent patterns in history, at least modern history. Revolutions, for example, have a way of running away from their authors. The French Revolution of 1789 began with the simple and moderate act of calling the Parliament. The 1917 and 1989 Russian Revolutions began with the moderate, pragmatic reformers Kerensky and Gorbachov. Who then foresaw the ultimate consequences? This is not to suggest that Britain is facing a conventional political revolution, but that the consequences of the present cultural conflict may be far-reaching and largely unforseeable.

The prospect of a post-Christian cultural revolution or cultural collapse of this type is certainly a new thing in the Anglomorph world. Tradition has provided one framework of values.

Christianity throughout the West has provided another framework of values whose central command, "Love one another", has, however imperfectly it has been obeyed, ameliorated even the darkest times. It has institutionalised ethics of nobility, charity and self-sacrifice. When Rome collapsed into the Dark Ages, Christianity provided a safety-net in which much was saved, including the cultural assets which made eventual recovery possible. It is hard to see the present Christian churches in a society like Britain fulfilling such a function in the event of cultural collapse, though some of their institutions may provide isolated pockets of refuge. The education system and culture seem to be producing — and this for the first time in actual fact as distinct from rhetorical prognostications — a generation of illiterate atheists. It is easy to break eggs without making an omelette.

At the time of writing — July 1998 — many of the underlying trends in the British economy are not good and serious economic problems regarding inflation, interest-rates and an over-strong pound seem a distinct possibility, even before considering the economic dislocation which may attend joining a single European currency. Britain and British society and culture have survived difficult economic times before but it is legitimate to wonder how well it may do so when those other, non-economic, cultural institutions which have provided the traditional structure and values of British life have come under such comprehensive attack.

We have taken little notice of how quickly things have changed. Thatcher as mentor and encourager of Reagan stiffening his resolution to destroy the Evil Empire almost as Henry V stiffened the troops as Agincourt, looks suddenly very distant, and like the last towering of a dying candle-flame. Valour? Nobility? Honour? Faith? Obedience? Sacrifice? Fortitude?

As I have tried to show here, this is a matter that goes far beyond politics as that term is now generally understood. We appear to be seeing in New Britain the government/ Nomenklatura-sponsored destruction of traditional culture, in conjunction with the erosion of social, religious and aesthetic values, in a way that is quite unprecedented.

And what rough beast, its hour come round at last, slouches towards Greenwich to be born?

*   *   *

There may be happier developments: while I believe Britain is in a deep cultural malaise, exacerbated by the cultural-warfare proclivities of the present government and Nomenklatura, cultural malaises are not necessarily incurable. It plainly has enormous cultural resources and resiliance.

If there is whisper in the air that "Resistance is useless!" it is one which conservatives should close their ears to. Rather, they should look to their own rich storehouse of tales of hope and heroism, renewal and valour.

The immediate tasks for cultural conservatives include rediscovering the value of connectivity. Politics, media and culture have always been connected in the most essential way and this has never been more true than now. Cultural conservatives need to recognise the profound extent to which the political is connected to the cultural.

In discussion with all manner of cultural conservatives in Britain over ten months of 1997-98, I have been most struck by their disconnectedness not merely from the programme and values of New Labour but also from each other, their feeling of aloneness and their ignorance of their own natural allies. Writers and other conservative intellectuals, for example, tend to be frequently lonely, isolated and ignored, sometimes seeing even one another as rivals when a little mutual self-help might magnify the influence of each enormously. *The Organisational Weapon* and Lenin's *What is to be Done* may still contain some lessons. Unless cultural conservatives — not merely the politicians of the Conservative Party — learn the value of organisational connectivity the future for them is bleak.

This should not, for conservatives, be a matter for despair but a challenge. This a conflict unlike any that preceded it, but there are still two sides. Evelyn Waugh (I quote from memory) once wrote to the effect that: "The spirit of the age is the spirits of those who comprise it, and the greater dissent from conventional fashion the higher the probability of diverting it from its present ruinous course."

There is already a certain dream-like quality about Britannia Year Zero and, looked back on from the standpoint of a few years ahead it may seem to have faded like a dream.

Surprising turns of the wheel are the rule rather than the exception and tomorrow automatically belongs to no-one.

The Author:

Hal G P Colebatch has a PhD in Political Science and is the author of 11 previous books. He is also a lawyer.

Index